Bunny has enjoyed many déjà vu and supernatural experiences throughout her lifetime. She has met many gifted people who have been able to see in the past as well as in the future. Among them are the late Torkum Saraydarian and Rev. Terrye Powell, and of current, Yvonne Ryba. These gifted metaphysicians have been of historic inspiration to her. Bunny channeled this book through prayer, meditation, and by listening to classical music.

To my late mother, Catherine Marie Brown Simpson; to my son, Taharqa Hannibal Simpson-Davis; and to God, all of whom provided immense inspiration for this book.

Bunny

SPIRITUAL FLIGHTS

A Look from the Past to the Future!

AUSTIN MACAULEY PUBLISHERS™

LONDON • CAMBRIDGE • NEW YORK • SHARJAH

Ordering Information:
Quantity sales: special discounts are available on quantity purchases by corporations, associations, and others. For details, contact the publisher at the address below.

Publisher's Cataloging-in-Publication data
Bunny
Spiritual Flights: A Look from the Past to the Future!

ISBN 9781643786131 (Paperback)
ISBN 9781643786148 (Hardback)
ISBN 9781645368335 (ePub e-book)

Library of Congress Control Number: 2019909673

The main category of the book — SELF-HELP / Personal Growth / General

www.austinmacauley.com/us

First Published (2019)
Austin Macauley Publishers LLC
40 Wall Street, 28th Floor
New York, NY 10005
USA

mail-usa@austinmacauley.com
+1 (646) 5125767

Chapter One
Truth Is Stranger Than Fiction

Mimi's Parlour and a Creole Funeral

In my aunt's parlour in the heart of New Orleans, 2532 Louisiana Avenue, I listened to "grown folks talking." Quietly, like a mouse in most familiar quarters, I sat, trying not to make my breathing heard while a variety of topics flowed past my young ears. One in particular that arose quite frequently for discussion curiously followed the last tune in the funeral band, usually a song of high celebratory jazz, like Louie Armstrong's "Oh When the Saints Go Marching In." Creole people in my clan believed that death in a family was most always a mysterious signal of a future birth and because of that belief a party followed the funeral, replete with foods the passing person enjoyed in this lifetime, hi-balls with whiskey, beer, wine, games of bridge, dominoes and of course jazz music.

My first funeral experience was with Mimi's husband, my Uncle George, a very handsome man, chocolate in color, straight black hair and beautiful dark brown eyes. He was so handsome he could have adorned any GQ or Esquire magazine ad! He was always fashionably dressed in one of the many suits he owned. In the summer, he wore a French straw hat and in the winter a light wool derby. Uncle George

7

was debonair, well-mannered, highly educated, and a voracious reader. He smiled confidently with everyone and was known as a man with a passionate heart. Uncle George supervised the "Projects"; small quarters of housing for the poorest of poor in New Orleans and its inhabitants sung his praises during his funeral. He was thought to be fair, honest, and a person of the Christ consciousness. Unlike the rest of us, he was a Protestant belonging to the United Methodist Church yet he believed in the sanctity of all professed religions and administered equal treatment to all people regardless of their belief or non-belief. I found it curious that his casket lay open in Mimi's Parlour prior to the funeral that day and I was terrified of passing by it. That morning as we drank our chicory-laden coffee, I was forced to pass by his casket and make the sign of the cross quickly, because the hearse had come and the band was assembling outside of Mimi's house. The band played very solemn music on the way to the church and by our arrival time we were all drenched from our tears of his passing. At the end of the ceremony we rode to the cemetery and buried him. On the way back to Mimi's house, the band played jubilantly and everyone's spirit was lifted somewhat. It was as though we had skipped to a different zone of reality, Uncle George was no longer in the physical and all who knew him shared happy remembrances of his life over Creole food, drinks, sweets, and of course jazz music.

Sister Dorsey

Many weeks had passed since Uncle George was laid to rest and this particular morning's enclave of chatter included vibrant exchanges between my mom; Cat, Mama Blanche; my grandmother, Mimi; my aunt, Maude; my most beautiful French godmother and the elegant and informed Sister Dorsey, who as my mom's godmother was attuned with world affairs as a result of her travels to foreign countries. Sister Dorsey enjoyed quite a reputation because of her knowledge, wisdom, and upscale residence in the French Quarters that placed her amidst people from all over the world. Sister Dorsey was a freckled faced woman with Irish red skin and always wore a turban, just a peak of her straight copper red hair showed. In all of my years of knowing her, I had to imagine what her hair looked like laying underneath those turbans. She had many turbans to match every haute couture outfit that seemed to lie perfectly upon her tall slim body. She was extremely tall, slender and her conformation as mother always exclaimed was "exquisite." Sister Dorsey resembled a modern day super model and the clothes she wore commanded the eyes of everyone in the room to turn around and gaze at a sophisticated spectacle of a gorgeous female. Sister Dorsey taught us to dress for the importance of the occasion when in eyesight of the public. "Your dress and mannerisms are an indication of the spirit of your personal confidence. It sends a message to the onlooker that indeed I am special, take me not for granted," she would remind us. The morning of Sister's arrival, I had Mother put all of my hair ribbons in their correct places and was quite precocious about having my black patent leather shoes shined with Vaseline to the point where I could see my face reflected in them.

Sister had announced her coming days before so that all preparations could be made. I had come in early that morning from my usual chase of chameleons in Mimi's backyard to take my spot on the stairwell to hear this grand, well-educated messenger. I had received my demi cup of Café du Monde coffee with chicory, flavored with a heavy dosing of evaporated milk; the kind in the red and white can with the nice cow on the label, and I sat in tremendous anticipation of what the talk would be.

Sister began by asking the great Creator God, Lord Jesus, Lord Buddha, archangels, angels and all of the Ascended Masters to bless the discussion. After a syncopated "Aaahh Meeen," Sister called for the Big Bible. The Big Bible was different from all of the others Mimi had around the house because it detailed the amount of African blood all of the Creoles and Mulatto's had in our family for centuries along with who married whom, or in some cases where whites and blacks could not marry in New Orleans, who resided with whom. For example, my great grandmother Maime, who lived to be 98, resided with my great grandfather who had emigrated from France. My grandmother had lived with my grandfather, a Lithuanian Jew who owned a store during WWII and accepted many a promissory note for a bag of rice and red beans from people who needed food. Whenever the Big Bible was used, something important was about to be exposed.

Sister began in her melodic voice, stating she would translate the meaning of Hebrews, Chapter 7, and "this is what we will discuss this morning." Lots of *oh*s and *ooh*s

10

followed that announcement. She continued with serious green eyes, boldly stating that Abraham was blessed by Melchizedek, the High Priest, who was without father, or mother, without a known birth, or known death, but like the Son of God would be a priest forever. At 5 years of age, I didn't believe the stork theory, and I wanted to raise my hand and ask how Melchizedek got down here to earth if he had no mother or father, but I was of course confined to silence. Sister's ensuing words made chairs move and coffee cups clatter as she described that the mysterious Melchizedek was thought by many to be an earlier incarnation of Jesus. At this point I jumped off the stairwell, ran right up to Sister, and asked her, "What's an incarnation?"

My Grandmother Blanche grabbed my chin, looked me straight in the eyes, and whispered loudly in French, "*Oh mon cher, tu meurs et tu reviens.*"

"Exactly," sister chimed in with English, **"you die and you come back."**

Sister said, "This passage speaks of reincarnation. It is telling us Melchizedek came from the divine and he preceded Jesus. This is like a prediction of him coming back as Jesus. In simple terms, it is my belief, he later reincarnated as Jesus. Now how do we know this, because the bible makes a reference to another priest like Melchizedek coming back 'not based upon any law or any prescribed ancestry, but on the basis of the power of God, and his body was indestructible, because he rose on the third day.'" Sister paused, "Remember Jesus was born to the Virgin Mary through the Immaculate Conception and his lineage was questioned by many."

The discussion continued with pronouncements of people they knew who died, crossed over and returned in another incarnation and had similar characteristics, professions, and behaviors of those possessed in the last lifetime. Mother made some kind of remark about who I was prior to this lifetime. So much time had passed that I was half-listening, ready to go back outside to my chameleons. I only remembered mother's description of a tall, slim woman, who was her aunt, with long black hair, filled with humor in all of her bones. I regret I never asked Mother her name specifically. And now as I write this book, Mother is 92 in an assisted living home in Colorado, Eagles Nest, and tells me when I call everything is going nicely.

But what I did recall from that initial discussion was that one better be very good in each incarnation lest some horrible misfortune could occur that might greatly impair your personal peace and happiness. They discussed certain cats and dogs owned by folks and likened the ways of those animals to persons known who had misused the talents God had given them in a previous incarnation. Aside from that I remembered not wanting to come back as some animal that could not read, write or speak, which apparently they thought had been the fate of those people who committed severe violations against the ten commandments. Sister Dorsey had ended the discussion with a stern warning that God remembers and records everything. I was twirling around and dropped one my chameleons that took a hard fall on the concrete in Mimi's backyard. I recall thinking I hope God didn't feel I did it on purpose. I had so much fun dizzying myself twirling around and was in such a hurry, skipping too fast to get to Mimi's back door when I heard Sister Dorsey had arrived.

Chapter Two
Being Recorded

What Is St. Peter's Book?

Sister Dorsey had left a large impression upon my mind regarding God knowing your every thought, word, and deed. Yet I had no idea of how he did it. It did not take too long for me to get more information about that process. A future incident would lead me to explore the idea.

A Lesson in Thievery

It all began when I was in elementary school. I was persuaded by an older girl to get a large package of notebook paper for less money. The trick was to swap labels and place the large package of notebook that cost 50 cents into the smaller package of notebook paper with the label of 25 cents. We were both at the U-Totem store an equivalent to today's 7 Eleven or Circle K convenience stores. I blindly followed her orders, slipping the large package of notebook paper into the 25 cents label used for smaller packs. The storekeeper let us escape unnoticed. I thought to myself as we walked back home, *What a bargain!* Now I will have notebook paper for a couple of weeks and I can write my poems and do extra drawings. I was a very happy camper.

Unbeknownst to me, the storekeeper had phoned my dad immediately upon our departure. Her house was in the middle of our block and she said goodbye and went inside. I skipped the rest of my way home. By the time I got there, my father met me at the back door and I was sternly walked back to store to return the paper. My daddy told the storekeeper to keep my quarter for his trouble and I went home with no notebook paper and was forced to get on my knees in the backyard to pray. It was a hot summer day 98 degrees in Houston, Texas with 90% humidity. I found myself in quite an uncomfortable position. Daddy pulled out the lawn chair, sat down, and instructed me to recite One Hundred Hail Marys and One Hundred Our Fathers and to ask God for forgiveness because of my horrible deed. Secondly, I had to plead to St. Peter to keep this incident of thievery out of the "good book." Daddy sat for a couple of hours as I knelt there in the scorching hot sun, praying my heart out and thinking all the while surely this is what "Hell" is like, as he checked off each and every prayer recital with his clicker in the palm of his hand.

I not only learned at the age of 9 years old never to steal again, but I also began to question everyone about the great book St. Peter held in his hand in certain religious pictures. I wanted to know its name and how could everyone's misdeeds on the planet earth be recorded in it. My rational mind told me the book would be bigger than the earth itself and bigger than the planet Jupiter, the largest planet in the cosmos. It wasn't until much later that a different picture would be painted in my mind, a more supernatural one.

Did the 100 Our Fathers and Hail Marys make amends for my deed of stealing notebook paper? Was the fact that my dad made me aware of how horrible it is to steal anything, coupled with my sorrowful attitude in 90 degrees of summer afternoon heat and humidity in Houston, serve as penance for what was already recorded in this massive record? Who knows? But for a nine-year-old, that became Alpha and Omega (the beginning and the end) and I never stole anything after that event.

Years later I was careful not to take home any company pens or paper. I never used a company credit card for any travel even when offered. I only conducted company business on my work computer and when cell phones surfaced, I always carried my own iPhone paying AT&T whatever I had to for company calls out of my own pocket. Indeed, a powerful life lesson was learned in the summer of 1958.

St. Peter's Book

In the Bible Philippians Chapter 4, Verse 5, a reference is made to a "book of life" by St. Paul. He insinuates in the passage there are those whose names are in the "book of life." Was this book the same as the "good book," I questioned myself? Was this reference to the book of life, the same as the "good book" or what metaphysicians refer to today as the Akashic Record?

I began to explore other passages in the bible and found references that pointed to each person appearing before the judgment seat of Christ. I had heard it mentioned many times before that when one gets to heaven, St. Peter has to look into the "book of life" to see if your name is there and if so, he would open the gates of heaven and let you walk through.

Was Daddy right? Is everything good and bad recorded so that upon physical death we appear before St. Peter, the keeper of the good book, or the Akashic Record that determines whether we enter into the gates of Heaven?

In many books on "the afterlife" there is a phrase, "I saw my whole life flash before me" mentioned by people dying or people who have died and actually come back to life. They describe the first event as a movie of their whole life flashing in front of them, lending credence to someone or something having recorded all of their lifetime events.

A professor and long-time mentor of mine who became "Professor Emeritus" at Arizona State University, was one of those who passed temporarily during a heart operation and returned to recant to his wife and I of how he saw his life flash before him like a movie after a massive heart attack—the first one which he survived. He was extremely well known throughout the university, the African-American community, and beyond the Phoenix metropolitan area. His genuine service to students and every person he came in contact with made him so well known. Whether individuals were seeking a job, trying to get accepted into ASU, or just a person with a problem this professor listened and tried to help. He became a living legend to the extent that if you were in need of any kind of wisdom, advice, or life decision-making, he was "the sage" to present your issue to for resolution. In astonishment, we listened and I thought was everything he had done in this lifetime recorded somewhere? When he died, would this information somehow be recorded into a "book of life" that

St. Peter is often seen holding? Is there a specific name to this book?

The Akashic Record

Wikipedia describes the Akashic Records as a collection of thoughts, events, and emotions encoded in a non-physical plane of existence called the Etheric Plane. Akashic comes from a Sanskrit word "aether" or atmosphere. Could it be that St. Peter's book is really the Akashic Record? If so, maybe all of those records St. Peter holds are in the "ethers" and not in some receptacle larger than any "iCloud" storage, and certainly not in a container as large as the planet Jupiter, as I had once imagined as a young girl. Maybe there is no need for a massive server or "iCloud" satellite to house the personal accounts of all of humanity and maybe there is more to an "Ethernet" than we humans could ever surmise or picture.

There is evidence however that the most well documented "Psychic" of modern time, Edgar Cayce, who lived from 1877 until 1945 accessed the Akashic Records to diagnose, treat, and heal individuals. The Edgar Cayce Institute today is alive and well in Virginia Beach, Virginia, in 2017.

The Akashic Records according to this institute is described as the "Book of Life." "More than just a reservoir of events," the Akashic Records contain every deed, word, feeling, thought, and intent that has ever occurred at any time in the history of the world for all individuals. What an awesome stream of universal consciousness this must be?

"Hence, as it has oft been called, the record of God's Book of Remembrance; and each entity, each soul—as the activities of a single day of any entity unfold in the material world—either makes same good or bad or indifferent impression is entered into the Akashic Records."

Edgar Cayce believed the Akashic Records copied every person's thoughts and actions and how they used their time in each physical manifestation or incarnation. He believed in each lifetime all people have a path to follow toward the service and advancement of mankind.

One might think this kind of Akashic Record as some sort of spiritual surveillance, like a "big brother watching over you." For many the idea is daunting to imagine that all thoughts, words, and actions of any and every human being born at any time in the history of our universe have been documented and recorded. It is crushing to think that all of the "malfeasance" created by thoughts and actions of earthly people have been recorded. We tend to live lives that we are familiar with. For many of us we have a "comfort zone" a "lane that we stay in" until something earth shattering occurs that makes us rethink how we react to our surroundings. We are taught to conform at an early age and as we grow we are told to "stay in your lane."

Staying in a lane of good behavior is perhaps wise advice in times like ours when lack of care for overall humanity propels some to move forward with negative and hurtful actions against those who are different, those whose beliefs don't quite parallel our own, or those who have more material wealth but may not give as freely as we think they should. Then there are those persons who suffer from mental imbalances, addictions, and a variety of unhealthy behaviors that may be incapable of understanding boundaries, guidelines, or structures, and upon occasion veer away from the lane into remarkable behaviors far away from positive human pathways. If indeed all of Human Malaise is documented into one Akashic Record, do we not lie in the mercy of one another's behavior in each reincarnation?

Chapter Three

Origins of Reincarnation

Coming Back

Tending Elephants

Mother and I talked often of the concept of reincarnation. She spoke so very fondly of the beautiful people of India and of her lifetime in India as a boy tending elephants, which may have explained her penchant for elephants. They were all over our house in various shapes and sizes, textures and colors, heights and widths. Visitors tended to marvel at her collection and she was quick to discuss the attributes of elephants. Mother always sat upright in her winged back chair informing them of the elephant's ability to show empathy and to use touch, sight, smell, and sounds to survive in their habitats. For Mother, the elephant was king of the jungle because other predators tended only to attack the smaller calves if unattended. "One had to be careful in tending to this large animal weighing 13,000 lbs because they had the intelligence to know if you were fearful around them," she remarked.

Her ease in describing the duties of an elephant boy amazed everyone. "It was important," as she continued in her low, slow New Orleans tone, enunciating her every word and syllable, "to cool the elephants off with water." Smiling and looking at the eyes of everyone straight away listening to her, she disclosed that the proper way of speaking to this massive animal was in very gentle tones. "Elephants carry heavy loads of goods across fierce jungle terrain and it is most necessary for the elephant to accept your closeness and your touch," she then bowed her head slightly to indicate closure of the topic. Most admired the collection with their eyes and for a few moments appeared as intoxicated as she during her theatrical gestures used while weaving her tale.

Few outside of Mimi's parlour knew of mother's belief of a previous life in India as a boy tending elephants. Mother belonged to a sorority whose symbol was that of an elephant, and most family friends associated her fondness of elephants with her sorority ties. Yet mother had an unusually special bond with her elephant statues and each one was polished, spoken to in her thoughts, and over the decades remained in their special places. One day when she was polishing the brass elephants and dusting the porcelain ones, I asked her if I had ever been an elephant boy. She responded, "You were my aunt in a lifetime, very tall, chocolate brown, slim, long black hair, and full of laughter in New Orleans." I remembered them describing me that time long ago in Mimi's Parlour but this one time when I inquired, mother seemed satisfied with the answer she'd given to me. I regret I did not pursue the issue further for a name, a date, and a timeframe of that kinship.

Am I My Father's Mother?

My father on the other hand often remarked that I looked like his Cherokee mother with a teaspoon of Irish, named Annie. Like me she had issues digesting food, had a keen interest in herbal cures, and was somewhat prim and proper. My cousin in San Francisco once told me she believed that Annie was a Celiac like myself but back in the day no one knew what that was and very few people had an opportunity to go to a doctor anyway. When folks look at Annie's picture, they see the resemblance in me.

My dad loved his mother tremendously and every step she took was a heavenly one in his eyes. She was without fault. She bore him on October 19, 1916, and did everything a mother could possibly do to feed three girls and two boys. I never heard my father speak ill of his mother, who managed during the great depression to place something in his lunch pail every day as he and his siblings walked several miles in their rural hometown to a schoolhouse. He told me, "She had hair like yours and steel gray eyes and was slimly built." The one picture I have, shows a pretty woman, with a nose and face very similar to mine with very light but somewhat saddened eyes. Her attire in that photograph was that of a prim and proper woman that seemed to be faintly on the brink of a smile. I never discussed reincarnation with my dad. He just often remarked that I looked like his mother. He named my older sister, Annie, after her. His mother died very early and in 1949 when I was born, Daddy was 33. He wanted to name me Jacqueline but mother thought that name was too common and chose to name me Gwendolyn Mary instead.

My Creole Folks

Mother taught me that the majority of people in New Orleans believed in reincarnation and it was never a foreign idea. Of course she had explicit details of how New Orleans and its inhabitants were different, more different than any other citizens in the United States. She taught me Creole people were special, in their manner of hospitality, in their gratitude for life that God had given them and by letting them be born Creole in New Orleans. She taught me that as a Creole, we were part French and like the French we appreciated fine china, the arts, music, education, and prized ourselves in the acceptance of all races of human beings. "The beauty of Creole People," she would say, "is that we come in all colors, from the blue-black indigo color of your Great-Grandmother Maime, to the pinky white of your Grandmother Blanche." In our New Orleans family, all of us were one and we quickly realized we were like bowls of Gumbo, all different ingredients made into one fabulous culture. We had no time for prejudice, for prejudice to us was just sheer unadulterated ignorance.

Our family's socio-psychological environment emphasized that the worst thing a human could do is to make any one soul feel unaccepted or unwelcomed. Creole people in my family did not judge others by all of the external glamor that seems to trap people in this world. They left judgment and evaluation of others up to the Lord. "We had a responsibility," Mother always said, "to help those who were without and as a part of our culture we are known to be cheerful, respectful, and dignified in our personal carriage." Mother believed in the concept of "*Tzedakah,*" which she saw as the very essence of Creole

Culture. "Never forget to entertain and be charitable to strangers, for in so doing some people have entertained angels unawares." For my Creole people in New Orleans, charity was innate in every good person and along with "*Laissez les bons temps rouler*" (let the good times roll). It was the Creole way of life.

The primary lesson I learned growing up, and spending all of my summers in New Orleans with Mimi, my aunt; Blanche, my grandmother; Sister Dorsey, mother's godmother; and Maude, my godmother, was to be good so that when you come back in another incarnation, your life would be pleasantly acceptable. I envisioned that idea as a part of my mission in each and every lifetime. Creole people believed in reincarnation, and believe it or not so did the early Christians and Jews.

Reincarnation Research

Recently in a study conducted by the Pew Foundation as reported by Thomas Ryan, in America Magazine, 51% of the world's population believes in Reincarnation and 25% of U.S. Christians believe in Reincarnation.

In the article "Reincarnation, Kabala, Judaism, Essenes, Pharisees," Walter Semkiw cites Flavius Josephus' belief in reincarnation, "Do ye not remember that all pure spirits when they depart out of this life obtain a most holy place in heaven from whence in the revolution of ages they are again sent into pure bodies."

It seems as though Flavius Josephus believed the soul was immortal and a divine part of man that existed within each human body. He saw the body being destroyed through the process of death yet the soul remained for the next incarnation if worthy. Josephus was a Jewish historian living through most of the first century A.D. He recorded in his writings that Reincarnation was widely acknowledged during his lifetime. One of his contemporaries living in Alexandria, Philo Judaeus referred to "re-embodiment" in his writings. Reincarnation comes from Latin and literally means, "entering the flesh again." The question to be asked is why would reincarnation be in a Latin origin of a word if it did not exist?

Reincarnation is a belief held by many in the world such as Buddhists, Hindus, Sikhs, Australian Aboriginals, Tribes in Central and West Africa and the majority of Native American Tribes in the U.S. like Navajo, Cherokee, Sioux, Lakota, Zunis, Gila River Indians, and Incas hold to this belief. "Scholars report that traditional Teutons, Druids, Eskimos, Celts, Gauls, the Pacific Peoples of Hawaii, and the Peoples of the South Sea, Japanese, and Eastern Russians believed in Reincarnation."

I was at dinner one Sunday at Chelsea's Kitchen in Tempe, late summer of 2017, with my good friends, a couple from Serbia. We were discussing reincarnation and the power of prayer. He disclosed that he had watched his father a Greek Orthodox Minister in San Francisco where he grew up, cast out a negative spirit through exorcism. He was 14 and recalled how his father was wringing wet after having prayed and prayed until finally the little boy was free of it. We discussed how in the early days 2,000 years ago and during the time of Constantine that people did believe in reincarnation. He stated he thought that was a belief in his family but never discussed. A prominent friend of mine;

a retired CEO of a Florida organization, disclosed she had always seen herself in a lifetime in UR about 4,000 B.C. Until I had mentioned I was writing this book, she had never said anything about it. I asked why? She said, "Oh Gwynn, I'm living here in Arkansas now and these people would be ready to hall me off to the funny farm."

Eyes Opened Wide in Our United States

The "Turbulent Sixties" and Seventies ushered into our homes via print media, television, and radio, changes through social movements that challenged what Americans historically believed in. Their homogenous livings rooms, schools, churches, civil, and social lives were shaken through a variety of social changes permeating the very fabric of what had been the "American Way of Life." For both urban and rural Americans these societal earthquakes shook many of their environmental beliefs passed down from generation to generation.

At the end of World War II, many women remained in the home, except those who were impoverished and those who sought to continue to work after the war mainly because it helped their families monetarily. Women worked because more were being accepted into the workplace. Many of these women sought to establish a career path.

However, the ideal role of the American woman was televised through the character of June Cleaver, wife of Ward Cleaver and mother of Beaver and Wally in "Leave it to Beaver." This popular family sitcom was seen in almost every home with a TV from 1957 to 1963. Regardless of race, economic status, and all of the other demographics categorizing American people in the '50s, this show epitomized home-life in the "Fabulous Fifties," one in which every American family should aspire to and hope to model. But something happened along the way that created a different yellow-brick road, and along the way differences in philosophy and ideas of what Americans are supposed to be stirred the status quo.

One devastating incident of change came with the assassination of President John F. Kennedy, leaving incoming President Lyndon Baines Johnson with a decision-making task similar in difficulty to that of President Abraham Lincoln; how to bring all facets of a society under one equal human rights umbrella that would unite the country rather than tear it apart.

Reincarnation is believed to be the activity of transferring one soul to another body after death. In other words the soul is transferred to a new embodiment. Was it this transfer of his soul into a new body in some future incarnation, that Dr. King had seen in a vision, that caused him to make the statement, "I've been to the mountain top and I've looked over, I've seen the 'Promised Land,' I may not get there with you, but I want you to know tonight that we as a people we will get to the 'promised land' and I'm so happy tonight. I'm not worried about anything, I'm not fearing any man, mine eyes have seen the glory of the coming of the Lord." This vision of what was to come may not have been visible to the average person at the time during the height of the civil rights movement but may have been Dr. King's ability to peer into his next reincarnation.

Americans began questioning the status quo through Dr. King's philosophy of non-violence based upon his study of

Gandhi and Eastern Philosophy. This caused more people to examine and become familiar with Eastern religions and thought. The continuance of the Civil Rights Movement under Dr. Martin Luther King made many Americans discuss what is equality?

The questions of what is right, what is moral, forced a number of individuals to look beyond traditional western beliefs and explore other cultural values held across the world. Dr. King's prophetic announcement, prior to his assassination, "I have been to the mountain top and I have seen white boys and girls playing with colored boys and girls," made many of us think how did he do this and how much truth was in his statement at a time riddled with racism? Did Dr. King see a future life? Was this experience, this great vision, an indication of reincarnation? It was well documented that Dr. King had studied Eastern Philosophy and it was well known that his writings were not those of a common man but of a man in tune with a type of spirituality that some folks were unable to fathom.

Dr. King continued his preaching of racial equality and non-violence and simultaneously another social movement occurred with the invasion of America by a song group called the "Beetles." As they sang, "All We Need Is Love," music, art, and self-help literature tied together the underlying foundations of a deafening social uprising. These social transformations apparently sustained an individual's investigation of concepts heretofore seemingly "far-out" from the ordinary way of life. Hippie sub-cultures, Vietnam War protests, societal emphasis of integration and inclusion, gay rights, life on other planets, meditation, planetary conservation and soul conservation became bell ringers of the "Dawning of the Age of Aquarius"; a New Age in the life of a still comparatively young America.

Knowing

During the seventies, globalization, exploration of new ethos, and technological developments in medicine and science all became forerunners of an advanced age in the United States. Americans realized their country had become a melting pot of immigrants in what was original Native American land. Religions, traditional, non-traditional, philosophies; both eastern and western, and people; white and non-white, were commingled into the human fabric based upon the principles of democracy, equality, and freedom of speech. Americans looked to other forms of "knowing," eating, fasting, and other ways of living to still their spirits. Being at peace with oneself and others became a priority for many segments of America's population.

In the early seventies, the Vietnam War disrupted white house politics and young college students protesting the war divided America once again. The hippies preached and practiced openly sex, peace, and demonstrations of love for all people. Mind exploration, through meditation, fasting, prayer, and clean eating were legitimized and segments of the American population viewed these practices as a way of attaining peace. The urge to develop faith not in what is seen but rather what is unseen, led some to a notion of the 6th sense; of knowing what is, what has been, and what is to be? People began to explore whether or not we come back into other lifetimes. There were those who flocked to psychic hotlines, desperately seeking a glimpse of a knowing beyond the traditional five senses. And then there was Timothy O'Leary who experimented with psychedelic drugs in search of "Nirvana." Millions of youth and young adults experimented with marijuana and others with more intense drugs trying to attain a permanent high. Yet some in search of a balanced emotional wellbeing, died in the midst of those drug quests. It became a fatal mission of some trying to know, of trying to feel the spirit within them and of trying see beyond what is?

For many Creole people in New Orleans this "knowing" and "spiritual insight" had been flowing from generation to generation without synthetic drugs. Creole people shared this commonality with the Native Americans and like the Native Americans the idea of seeing beyond the reality of the five senses has just been an acceptable way of life.

I remember once we were driving across a patch of land in the south and mother winced while watching out of the car window. She grabbed her chest and tears began to flow out of her eyes. Daddy asked if she was getting carsick. He pulled into a gas station where he had to fill up. The stop did not awaken my sister. I put my hands on mother's shoulders and asked what happened back there. She exclaimed, "Bunny, I see the spirits of all of the Confederate and Union soldiers who died there in the battle fields back there." I got out of the car and told Daddy Mother needed some soda water, perhaps a coca cola would do. Later on, after we arrived at my cousin's house, and while mother was unpacking my suitcase, she did tell me she could see the faces of the soldiers walking along the side of the road. They were sad and she felt the energy of death from the civil war battle there. It would not be until later when I learned about the "transference of energy" that I could fully understand mother's feelings at that point in time.

Chapter Four
Legitimacy of Reincarnation

Is Reincarnation Fact or Fantasy?

Is Every Lifetime the Same?

It is important that the idea of Reincarnation have legitimacy so to speak, albeit for those of us in the light it is perfectly acceptable. Why? Because we see it as a factor of "free will" given to us by the Creator. Perhaps reincarnation is not "what happens" in every case, a little understood law of nature, but nature's solution for how long it takes people to change. How with free will, we take our sweet time being in harmony with nature's creation, and so reincarnation gives us many chances to wipe the slate clean, like a real-life extended version of the movie, "Groundhog Day."

Perhaps more highly attuned and evolved spiritual beings are having experiences where they don't have to die and reincarnate. I wonder if someone like Mother Theresa who gave her entire life so unselfishly would have to come back to earth in another incarnation. Or if Abraham Lincoln, who had a premonition of his death or John F. Kennedy, whose short life positively impacted the lives of Americans and whose death was mourned by many nations; or Dr. Martin Luther King who seemed aware of his impending closure to this lifetime, are all mightily sacrificed souls. Must they too return for other life spans? Are martyrs destined to come back to another lifetime to continue their mission? Maybe it's not necessary for one to die, but helpful because "Death" so thoroughly wipes the slate of the soul clean.

If Reincarnation is a chance to start over, is it not a good tool? Rather than reincarnation being what all beings do, maybe reincarnation is a way for nature to give us more chances to fulfill our natural potential and to be of service to humanity. If so, heroines and heroes of whom we have many in the history of earth, have all demonstrated the need for us all to be good to one another in each and every lifetime.

Papa in the Sky

I recall some moments, after having left Seattle and 10 years of marriage, I was cleaning my apartment in Mesa, Arizona. It was a two-bedroom place upstairs and was near the job I had taken at Arizona State University. I had been up half the night trying to even out the bottom of our Christmas tree with a butcher knife to fit in the tree holder. Taharqa, my three-year-old son, sat up the entire night until I finally got that tree up and decorated. The man at the tree lot was drunk and had not cut it evenly. It took me until 3 am to get it into tree stand. The next morning, I was busy in the kitchen cleaning up the chipped pieces of the tree when I heard some Spanish phrases being spoken. I did not have the radio on a Spanish speaking station and to my surprise it was coming from the closet. Taharqa had gotten up a few minutes earlier and made his way into the coat closet. He was laughing and talking and speaking Spanish. He hardly knew English and I listened for several minutes unable to decipher what he was saying. Trying not to disturb him by opening the closet door, I stood outside of the closet listening through the keyhole and finally asked him "Boo, whom are you speaking to?" We had nicknamed him Boo as he delighted in hiding under the stairwell when we lived in Seattle trying to scare us, or treading ever so lightly on the floor that before you noticed he was right behind your back shouting, "Boo, I scared you." I kept talking to him through the keyhole, asking, "Boo, whom are you talking to?" He refused to answer and kept on with the conversation. Finally, I swung the door open and asked, "Boo, who are you talking to? You can tell me, I am your mom!"

He gave me a frustrating look and said, "Papa, in the sky." He then stormed out of the closet and shook his finger at me and said, "You wait till I am the dad again and you the baby." I was astonished and sat down at the kitchen table asking myself, "Now what just happened here?"

Ironically, this child has ruled over me since his birth and continued to do so throughout his childhood and early adulthood. He has always demonstrated unusual common sense and always made independent decisions. His dad who, subsequently, left Seattle to move to Phoenix to be near his son, always marveled at his early intelligence. I will take the memories of those moments of him in the closet, speaking Spanish to Papa in the sky, along with the fact that we had relatives of Mexican descent in this lifetime and in my father's lifetime, to my grave. I have coupled those memories with the Curiel Klan, who adopted him into their family upon first meeting him in this lifetime. Chris is and continues to be my son's best friend, and his sisters and brothers are Taharqa's sisters and brothers and his mom and dad are Taharqa's second mom and dad and I have become the second mom, Mama Gwynn, to all of the Curiel children and their children. Is this Karma?

Has Taharqa lived as a Mexican-American or Hispanic in a previous lifetime? Is this just coincidental that he would have such a strong tie and linkage with a Mexican-American family here in Arizona? Was it coincidental that I graduated from a college in New Mexico where my soul was at rest and is always at rest when I travel to New Mexico? Is it coincidental that we live in Arizona and in spite of the hot summers my soul is at rest here within a large Hispanic and Native American population?

While Taharqa is not my dad in this lifetime, he certainly acts like it. Who knows maybe he was my dad in a previous lifetime and maybe he will reincarnate and become my dad in a future lifetime as his little pointed finger stated 35 years ago? Are these and other incidents simply "coincidental" or is it really Karma?

Chapter Five

Reincarnation

Is Karma the Cause of Reincarnation?

What Is Karma?

The word "Karma" has its origins in the ancient language of Sanskrit. Sanskrit was spoken more than 3500 years ago and is related to Hinduism. As a point of reference it is estimated that the prophet Abraham lived 4100 years ago and early Jewish groups that followed Jesus believed in reincarnation and Karma, as did the "Gnostics." The Gnostics did not so much believe in after life but thought true believers in Christ, had to live a Christ like life. They also believed that souls reincarnated into different lifetimes to attain a level of Christ-like perfection. "You saw Christ, you became Christ. For this person is no longer a Christian but a Christ. If someone first acquires the resurrection, he will not die."

Is it through reincarnation that a person gains the ability in each cycle of life and death to become more like Christ? Jesus said, "Whoever drinks from my mouth will become like me; I myself shall become that person, and the hidden things will be revealed to him."

In John, Chapter 9, verse 1, the disciples are questioning Jesus regarding the sin of a blind man. They asked Jesus whose sin caused the man to be born blind? Was it his own sin or was it his parent's sin passed along to him? Implied within this question is that the blind man had "Karma" because of his previous incarnation or Karma was passed to him from his parent's previous incarnation.

Is it the accumulation of Karma that causes us to reincarnate to attain more "Christ-like" behaviors? Was Jesus' Death on the Cross a bad thing? Is being more Christ-like in our actions towards others and ourselves a bad thing?

Gnosticism differs from Western Christianity's rational for living a good life. Christianity tells us to live a good life is to earn a one-time entrance into heaven. Western Christianity teaches St. Peter guards the gates of heaven and is the one pictured holding a book, as we see him standing in front of heavenly gates in many artistic depictions. Many western religions teach that it is St. Peter holding the book and looking inside to see if one qualifies for a heavenly entrance. Have you ever wondered what this book really is and what does it contain? Some of us may have learned this book records everything you say and do as I did from my daddy at the age of nine.

Diana

After the heartbreaking loss of Princess Diana I wondered about reincarnation once again. Few of us really knew who she was, but all of us felt we had been touched by her spirit. How on any earth was it that all colors of people, all sexes of people, all nations of people felt her immense love through television and the media? How on earth did millions of humans feel as though a part of who they were and what they believed in was taken away so abruptly? Princess Diana was the world's royalty who showed every man/woman/child spirit on earth, what love really is? Her heavenly and divine grace was evident in her eyes, smile, the clothes she adorned, and more importantly the human cause projects she assumed. Diana touched, healed, and spread hope for those around the world whom many of us had forgotten and/or ignored in the economic human equation. She was poised both in speech and her rather demure behavior. Diana's aura was angelic that warmed us so much, that she became the universe's Princess. I questioned would she indeed come back into another lifetime having moved the very earth she was a part of forever so briefly? Were her deeds of compassion to every one she met enough to close the door to any other incarnation? Our world had never seen a "Diana" yet our world lost a part of the energy of its entire humanity in her abrupt loss.

References to Reincarnation in the Bible

The Gospel of Matthew, Chapter 16:13–14, alludes to numerous implications of reincarnation, specifically when Jesus questioned the disciples about who people thought he was? The disciples said that some thought he was John the Baptist. John the Baptist had been beheaded years before Jesus raised the question. Later in the Gospel of Matthew, Chapter 17, verse 13, Jesus states an assumption that John the Baptist may have been the prophet Elijah. Was this a hint at possible reincarnation when he told his disciples if they were OK by it, perhaps John the Baptist was the Elijah who was to come?

Clearly, Elijah preceded John the Baptist in birth. It doesn't appear that Jesus rejected the idea of reincarnation, nor does it appear that reincarnation was a foreign idea outside of the Jewish religion during the first century.

Other references in the bible imply not only reincarnation but also the idea of "Karma." It is a broadly held belief that early Christians, Jews, and those believers of the Sacred Sutras, and Buddhist understood reincarnation. But what about the idea of "Karma" what is it? Do we accumulate Karma every time we reincarnate, as implied in the disciples questioning of Jesus about the blind man?

Chapter Six

Is Karma Punishment?

What Are Karmic Lessons?

You Are What You Think You Are?

Shuh (an expression used by my Mimi, my aunt, meaning to give pause to think), we must ask ourselves how many times we harbor negative thoughts in our minds about people, conversations, things, and objects? For the most of us, it is second-place to judge and evaluate someone we even see for a split second, let alone someone we feel may have hurt us in some way.

The self-talk in our minds can range from comical to vicious depending upon our reaction to an incident or a long-term hurt we have allowed to find a home in our comfort zone. We may have angry thoughts about a divorce when a partner leaves us. Angry thoughts can grow tentacles which we use on any given day, at any given moment, to remind ourselves how a person treated us, devalued our self-worth, or emotionally or physically abused us.

Sometimes we repeat bad experiences in relationships through the same kind of hasty decisions, judgments, and evaluations of our circumstances and the people we meet.

We will repeat the behavior of conjuring up old hurts until we actually let them go and begin to heal ourselves. Mother always told me, "Be still and know there is God." She reminded me constantly that in being still God would send a guardian angel to place the correct thoughts into my consciousness. But if my consciousness were full of evil and negative thoughts the window for the guardian angel to enter would be closed.

Vanity Has Always Been Man's Enemy

I can recall one young man who was considered one of the most handsome men at the university. Typical, California beach boy look with curly frosted blond hair on a more than 6 ft. frame. He got the second look by young women every time he strolled across campus. He had his pick of lovely young women and during his years there engaged in a great number of sexual relationships. He graduated, obtained a Ph.D., and began a teaching career with a small private college for more than a decade. It was reported by others that he dated his female students, some who had entered college at the ages of 16 and 17 years old. It was believed that he continued that practice well into his 40s. He entertained these under-aged women at his home. He mentioned to some friends he was quite surprised that even though he was in his 40s, he was able to date young girls without any protest from their parents. At one point he had a sexual relationship with a nun for several years and found it fascinating that she never disclosed anything about it. This man, like many other men, looked for the unusual, always wanting something different. What some parts of society felt to be unconventional practices in sex, his selection of practices and people to engage in sex with varied tremendously. He appeared to make a sport of the sexual relationship, never becoming serious and always moving forward when the grass seemed greener or when chance afforded him the opportunity to engage in sex with someone new or different. California is a live and let live state; a freewheeling environment where having an unconventional lifestyle is acceptable. It was reported years later that he left the college where he was teaching under some cloud of scrutiny. He passed in his early 50s of heart attack. Did his heartless behaviors of a sexual hunter come to rest in his actual heart? For every physical action is an emotional response action in our bodies. Did his accumulation of Karma in this lifetime end his life prematurely?

Fast-forward to a man in his mid-fifties who had been involved in casual sexual relationships his entire life. He moved from the south to the east coast where he and a female business partner joined forces. He was still quite handsome and eventually began living with the woman in a multi-million dollar home. He had sold his properties and together they resided in a wonderful estate. She had inherited a great deal of money and had children from a previous relationship. They traveled the world and seemingly were enjoying life. Something happened that ended the partnership. It was thought she cheated on him and left him. He told others she had moved back to her native country. Later on he said they could not agree on a city to live in. After a lifetime of hurting other women, he found himself in quite unfortunate circumstances after that and now in his 70s is living in an apartment thousands of miles from the million-dollar mansion, the upscale lifestyle, and the world travels.

Was this karmic payback for all of the hearts broken from his promiscuous past? Does Karma present itself in a current lifetime as in the case of this gentleman? Will there be other karmic debts he will face in other lifetimes as a result of his actions in this present incarnation?

Fear of Being Alone

One young, vibrant, beautiful auburn haired woman living in the northwest was married to a very successful businessman. She met him at a college lecture at the University of Washington. She was a marketing and advertising agent, degreed, quite bright, and very attractive, with a high-energy personality. She was perfect for her profession and quite successful in her own right. She was enthralled with the idea of marrying the most handsome and debonair man that she could. She wanted a man who had the potential to give her all of the material things she desired. Her husband's company expanded from the United States to China. After a while his travel increased and often she found herself alone with a young son. When the husband did return from long trips, he purchased material things for her; expensive clothes, shoes, and jewelry, yet his intimate moments with her began to wane as he became more and more involved in his business interests. One day while doing the laundry on one of his return trips, she noticed something peculiar, stains in strange places on his underwear. On another occasion when preparing for dinner she noticed the food she was to cook had been tampered with. She decided not to cook it and threw it out. She began inquiring about his growing business and he was very reluctant to give her any information about his involvement and appeared irritated every time she asked. He was an extraordinarily handsome man, the kind that would adorn the front cover of GQ Magazine. She noticed significant changes in his already impeccable appearance, specifically the ultra-smoothness of his skin. Eventually, his stays at home with her gradually declined and he had absolutely no interest in his son. She finally put two and two together and inquired as to whether or not he had another woman in his life. He continued leaving significant clues in his laundry. The cologne found in the scent of his shirts was not that of a woman. The phone calls to her home were not from a woman, always a man who never left a name or message. Finally after one severe confrontation with him, he disclosed his lover was the man he began expanding the business with in China. She was devastated that he had moved on from their relationship to one with his male business partner. He left her with the home and a specified amount of money in the bank. She sold the home and moved back to her hometown in New York to find support from her parents and family.

She felt abandoned and began feeling challenged that her femininity was not enough for a man. She developed a hatred for bi-sexual and homosexual men, totally blaming herself for a failed marriage. Over and over in her mind she questioned how could she have been so foolish, in not noticing the signs sooner. Indicators of his behavior, the late night phone calls, the unwillingness to speak with her, the lack of attention to her son, all of which were issues she glossed over, thinking surely she was the greatest partner he could ever have. She felt she was being punished and wondered what sin had she committed in her past to lead to such personal devastation and such horrible Karma.

The question becomes, is Karma always something that punishes us for behaviors from the past or can we accumulate Karma through decisions of the present?

This young woman failed to remember that her main goal was to marry a rich businessman, not any businessman, but an extraordinarily handsome one! She wanted an expensive home, and she was enamored with status and wealth. She had always used sex as a way to get expensive shoes and handbags in her relationships prior to meeting her husband and felt these material acquisitions defined her as an important person of means. She had not spent a lot of time dating and getting to know the man who would become her husband, simply because when he appeared, she felt he would be a great conduit to the material things she desired at an early age in life. Is Karma linked to personal intent? Is good Karma linked to both good and selfish intention?

Once again this young woman formulated the same goals and set out to find another man of status. She began dating again and found herself in an out of relationships and sometimes dating two or three men simultaneously in search of the material lifestyle she hungered for. Many of these relationships were purely casual sexual relationships in nature because she felt if a man could have fun, so could she. Besides she had no faith in a man's ability to respect and honor sex in a relationship having recently been divorced under such negative circumstances. She continued to blame herself for the failure of her first marriage, ignoring the fact that her prime motivation for a relationship was based on her need for money and status.

In running in and out of nightclubs, she ran upon another wealthy man. He was not good looking was not tall and was not particularly interesting. She convinced herself because he had a good business and could provide her with the material things and status she desired, he was a safe bet. She quickly married him. As her career took off, he became jealous and began to abuse her. Without realizing it, she found herself in a similar situation as the first marriage, emotionally abused and suffering from physical abuse as well. One night the second husband came home and raised his fist to strike her, only to meet the fist of a much taller young man, her son. She left the home, son in tow, and left her hometown of New York for a southern city. She continued to jump quickly into sexual relationships that did not last. She had not taken time to evaluate her motives and now with an adult son she was more anxious to find a partner. She is no longer the size two, petite young woman she had been twenty-five years ago. Desperation has now set in in her life and it appears this woman cannot function without a spouse in her life.

Sometimes when we don't take time to heal from a hurt and we hold ourselves to the holy trinity of guilt, shame, and blame, is when we fail in relationships. We may lack the internal mechanisms to evaluate our motives and ourselves. When we fail to consider "intent," there is a tendency to repeat the lesson we should have learned initially. She later admitted she had been artificially inseminated and her son was not the son of the first husband.

Did this woman ignore clues from the very beginning of this relationship with the first husband? Was she so happy to have a debonair, handsome, and successful husband that she overlooked other important things in a relationship? Was she, unbeknownst to herself, a willing cover for a gentleman whose orientation was not that of a heterosexual male to begin with? Was she so insecure that she felt she could not exist on her own and took the first chance at remarriage that she could? Had she really examined her self-talk to see if her reality was really real or did she have a fantasized notion of what a married life consisted of? Was she continuing to create the same kind of Karma by not changing her behavior and approach to formulating successful partnerships? Is Karma passed from one lifetime to another? Do we create Karma with negative behaviors in any incarnation?

Is Karma created through our mental and physical actions? Is Karma associated with intent? If we act with intent that is not harmful, do we still create Karma or do we go unscathed? Is Karma based upon our ability to maintain virtuosity with good intent?

Chapter Seven
How Do We Reincarnate?

Those We Know

Do We Reincarnate with Those We Knew in Other Lifetimes?

In my Creole culture, we were taught we reincarnate with loved ones we've had attachments to in previous lifetimes. Those lifetimes may have been lived in other countries because we are not always the same race or sex in each incarnation. Perhaps this is why my son shook his finger at me and said, "You just wait till I get to be the daddy again," after I opened the closet door on him while he was speaking Spanish to Papa in the sky. There are those who believe we reincarnate with many of the same people we have known in other lifetimes.

Oftentimes it is no accident that we meet and run into individuals whom we have an immediate connection and comfort level with.

Children Can Recall Other Lifetimes

Ian Stevenson, M.D. Psychiatrist who died in 2007, was a professor at the University of Virginia. Over his career, Stevenson compiled and studied approximately 3000 cases involving children who spontaneously remembered past lives in detail. Dr. Stevenson traveled to the scenes of the contemporary and past lifetimes to interview witnesses to assess details provided in these past life accounts. In about 1200 of these cases, the past lives of these children could be factually validated.

A very important observation made in reincarnation research is that individuals can change religion, nationality, ethnic affiliation, race, and gender from one lifetime to another. "Most wars are based on differences in these cultural markers of identity. One of the most powerful reincarnation cases that demonstrate change of religion, nationality, and ethnic affiliation from one incarnation to another is the case of Anne Frank. Walter Semkiw, using Dr. Ian Stevenson's research, believed Anne Frank reincarnated in Barbro Karlen. Their physical features are quite similar. Anne Frank was persecuted and died in a concentration camp as a Jew, while Barbro was born into a Christian family in Sweden. If the German people at the time of WW II knew that one could be born Jewish in one lifetime and Christian in another, then perhaps the Holocaust may never have happened, believes Semkiw." Both Barbro and Frank closely resemble each other.

Similarly, when Jewish Israelis realize they can reincarnate as Muslim Palestinians and vice versa, Protestants can reincarnate as Catholics, Islamic terrorists know that they can reincarnate as Christian Westerners, and Shiites know they can return as Sunnis, then violence based on these different affiliations will be mitigated.

"Dr. Stevenson reported in his research on the 1200 cases of past lives of children that body size and height may differ from one reincarnation to the other, facial features can remain the same throughout various incarnations."

Daddy always said I looked like his mother. His mother was Cherokee with a teaspoon Irish, he used to say. Ironically, we are quite similar in appearance. I am a Celiac in this lifetime. His mother had digestive problems and his first cousin in San Francisco told me his mother suffered just as I did after eating. I was diagnosed as a Celiac and I often wondered if my grandmother suffered from something similar. Daddy was born in 1916 and his mother died late in the '30s. I was born in 1949 in this lifetime. I feel quite at home with my Native American brothers and sisters and always felt I lived many life times as a Native American. In repeated dreams I saw myself as a Squaw walking through Florida with a son on my back. In New Mexico and Utah, the vibrations of having lived in those areas have been extremely strong. When I traveled to Russia at the age of 19, I walked into a Russian Orthodox Church in Moscow where I had so many déjà vu experiences, I felt I had lived there before. Later returning to Belgrade in 2005 and to Budapest in 2017, I experienced the same type of comfort level, feeling quite at home. In my very first visit to Paris, I felt I had finally come home. Walking through Versailles was one of the most eerie experiences I've ever encountered.

If we come back as different races of people in different lifetimes, should cultural identity continue to be points of difference in our societies?

Chapter Eight

Evaluating

Judging a Book by the Cover

In the Western World the Outside Matters

We so casually judge and evaluate people or do we have cultural and environmental filters that prevent us from making decisions that would render a circumstance more beneficial to our real needs? We are all influenced by material goods, societal status, and expectations imposed upon us by relatives, friends, and more importantly, the media. In modern times the media plays a huge role in defining the standards of the society we live in. For example there is little reverence for older citizens and senior citizens in American culture, they tend to be cast aside especially if poor and on a fixed income. There is a heavy emphasis upon youth, beauty, financial independence, and living large. All of these variables are equated with success. The media ads tell us we should never grow old or look old. And if we do look old, there are Facelifts, Botox, and other accoutrements that can keep us from ageing. There are exceptions to average citizens and those exceptions seemingly are those who seem not to age and are shown in advertisements. The sixty-year-old female who can hike mountains, run a marathon, and fit into a size 2 dress does not mirror the majority of sixty-year-old females in our country. Few middle or working class women can afford to spend hours in a gym, maintain shots of Botox, or pay for a Facelift.

In era where food is preserved for years in a grocery store warehouse, the majority of Americans are aging from severely depraved nutritional environments. Typical jobs afford American workers two weeks of vacation per year. Many Americans are working two jobs to make ends meet. Very few Americans are able to save as the cost of living for the majority of working people make it difficult to save. In the '80s, President Reagan spoke of generations of families living under one roof due to the changes in the American economy. Today, adult children are staying home with parents longer because of an inability to purchase a home or pay for apartment living. Those young adults who do live away from home oftentimes have roommates to assist with the costs.

Although clean eating is becoming more and more an acceptable alternative to "fast food," few working Americans can afford to purchase fresh vegetables and fruits, let alone bear the costs of organic vegetables and fruits. Food with additives and preservatives, the lack of fresh air and exercise, job stress, and the difficult task of living in an unfavorable economy make it impossible for a lot of families to manage a healthy lifestyle. Emotional and physical stress along with genetics and the inability to purchase healthy foods, find time for proper exercise, or more importantly access to good health care all dictate the number of wrinkles in a person's skin.

Poor air quality, inadequate income and resources, and poor health, all contribute to a premature aging process. Vitamins and supplements, fresh food, comfortable and humane living circumstances, access to education, travel, and the ability to de-stress as advertised through today's media are not tools available to the average American. While some are able to "find their Hallelujah," the majority of human beings do not have time to question why things happen to them, they are simply just trying to survive.

Often the question of why I am here and can I change my life path of circumstances, comes only after tragedy, disease or an unforeseeable setback. People tend to "stay in their lane," remain in that comfort zone with those who are like them, for those who are different are sometimes viewed as "threats." When a threat becomes too overwhelming, some people turn to drugs or other avenues that further jeopardize their ability to lead healthy lives. Racism, religious ostracizing, intolerance of others who profess different sexual orientations or different philosophies about life should not separate us from being kind to one another. Our mother earth has within it enough resources for all children and all adults to live in humane conditions with clean water and fresh food. We have technologies that can improve and enhance our environments and produce jobs. We must begin to acknowledge there are a number of creative ways to eliminate disease and restore health to planetary people. We must respect our farmers and agriculture and produce food without preservatives, chemicals, and harmful drugs aimed at stretching shelf life in a grocery store warehouse. The lack of fresh and natural food is the number one cause of disease and poor health, coupled with stressful living circumstances. What is important are not the differences but rather how do we live in harmony with one another, by respecting all of humanity, respecting ourselves, and respecting a higher power other than ourselves who governs all of us on planet earth.

Chapter Nine
Comfort Zones

Mainstream Versus Other Stream

We Like What Makes Us Comfortable

Traditionally, this country has scorned the unhealthy, the mental, economic, and socially disadvantaged person no matter what the gender is. Women have historically been seen as the weaker sex, people of color have historically been viewed as less than human, and therefore less worthy than people of white descent, and people whose sexual orientation is different have not been viewed as a part of mainstream society.

For the most part, Americans find their comfort zone and stay in it, generation after generation. This is particularly true for Americans in more rural areas whose family traditions and beliefs remain unchanged regardless of educational enhancements achieved in other parts of western civilization. They teach their children these boundaries of their personal comfort zone and when family individuals stray from those boundaries, they are sometimes no longer acceptable to the family group. They may be ridiculed and sometimes become estranged from the families they were born into. With exposure to other cultures comes new ideas, innovative ways of thinking, acceptances of other cultures and family rituals. For many rural American families this type of "new age" thinking is viewed as a threat, and labeled as "the work of the devil" or irreligious.

Once when I was in undergraduate school at a Catholic University in the southwest, I met a fellow from Florida, of German descent. I fell in love, continued my studies, and began envisioning a future. I had transferred to the university having spent my first two years at a Catholic College in Michigan and after having traveled to England, Germany, France, Sweden, Denmark, and Russia. Right after a holiday break, I noticed the young man walking across campus holding hands with another female student. I walked away from the previous months in total silence, never questioning what happened and never experiencing any amount of closure to that relationship.

Four decades later, this gentleman caught up with me by calling my sister and leaving his number. By email he informed me his mother had passed away. He disclosed I had almost given his mother a heart attack. I inquired how could that be possible, I had not known his mother in this lifetime? He responded, "Oh silly, that happened when I told my mother I was dating a 'vanilla girl.'" I was non-white, a "vanilla girl" he termed me, far different from the "Creole Label" I had grown up with. It became obvious at that moment he had chosen not to stray from those family values of "white supremacy," albeit Catholic in religion; religion did not trump racism in the year 1969. But exposure and time do and can evolve into progressive thought. I am happy to report that we are still friends.

Remaining in comfort zones that discount the values of other cultures, races, religions, and societal beliefs creates massive divisions between people in general and among families. Hatred of other religions, people of other nationalities, and sexual orientations can bring much harm. Why, because all of those differences are perceived as threats to those who remain in their comfort zones of being separate and apart generation after generation from a larger humanity.

Comfort zones can only be changed through education and exposure to other people and other cultural practices. Unfortunately too many people see globalization as a threat to their comfort zone of perceived economic status. People of color are viewed as a threat to the comfort zone of race supremacy. Cultural, political, and philosophical differences are a threat to the comfort zone of class and identity.

What happens if we continue to stay in our limited comfort zones? What happens if we never learn the karmic lessons of creating a peaceful humanitarian earth?

Will earth continue to be a paradise hosting reincarnation parties for eternity? How long will the act of reincarnation continue to provide opportunities for world peace? And what if we don't get it right, collectively, as a global planet earth, we could very well ignore the invisible forces of nature and as an inhumane people, blow ourselves up during one of our cyclical "chances." That could well be the end of the cycle of reincarnation on earth. We may not have another opportunity for mother earth to repair itself and get ready for another party. Is the understanding and acceptance of what it means to be "human" on the planet earth the karmic lesson that all of us in America and other countries must learn?

What happens when bad things happen to good people? Is that a karmic lesson? Or is it oftentimes the transference of energy of someone who has bad Karma to someone who is quite innocent? Is that what happens when a good person is killed by a drunk driver? Or a jealous person sets a death trap for someone going on with daily life? Was it Karma for the church people in Charleston, SC, to lose their lives at the hands of a young person confused about race and superiority and full of hatred for people whose skin color was different? Was it Karma that caused the Las Vegas shooter to kill so many innocent people? Was it the Karma of the veteran who shot up the members of the small church in Texas? Was it Karma that generated death in the Orlando nightclub? Was it karma when a shooter entered the churches in New Zealand or in Pittsburgh that killed members of the synagogue? Or was it the transference of one person's negative energy to others via social media, promoting white supremacy?

Dinah

I met a young woman from the east coast seeking a job in my hometown where I was working with a transit system. She lacked a degree but had such great communications and employee relations' skills that I was impressed with her presence and infectious laugh. This young lady did not let an early high school pregnancy prevent her from obtaining her diploma. She accepted the responsibility and began working to support herself and her daughter. I admired her persistence and will to make a better life for herself and daughter. She moved to Houston and applied for a position. I was interviewing for an administrative assistant and hired Dinah. She made herself invaluable and won everyone over as she met young, old, unionized, non-unionized, degreed, not degreed, single, married employees from a workforce of 8,000 people throughout the transportation system. Her writing skills were excellent and her problem-solving and analytical skills even better. Every department head asked me, "Gwynn, where did you get her from?" I would always respond, "Heaven sent" to all who inquired. She learned the business of transportation quickly and helped us build a human capital management system that was "servient centered" and cost effective. She was good in sizing up the right candidates to hire and knew the right questions to ask to bring out the best in applicants. Her reputation grew and grew throughout this large transportation system that had five facilities at the time. As we promoted one Employee Relations Representative to Employment Manager, a vacancy occurred. Everyone in our human resources department asked if we could promote her to the vacant position. Department heads asked and eventually the General Manager inquired about the possibility of promoting Dinah. I was overwhelmed by the response as I had already determined she was the right person for the job but had my work cut out in getting her convinced to apply for the job. I was the Assistant General Manager and could not ask her to apply. But one such engineer who came down every day to take me to coffee in the Tenneco Tower could. He was a handsome Italian man that I missed out on. He liked me but I wasn't sure, as I had been out of the dating game. Dinah used to ask me why do you think he comes down here every morning to buy you coffee? I kept worrying about my son but as I look back he would have made a wonderful stepfather. One morning we talked and I asked Leo to speak with Dinah. He said, "Certainly, I will ask her for coffee and encourage her to apply." Apply she did, and I left the screening and interviewing to others to keep my hands out of the employment process. Dinah won the job hands down and assumed her role as Employee Relations Representative.

A few months later, Dinah met a gentleman, Matthew, and they fell in love and were married. Matthew was anxious to begin a family because he had no children of his own. As they attempted, Dinah failed to get pregnant. She went to see an OBGYN who informed her she had a fibroid and that needed to be removed to pave the way for a pregnancy. Dinah and Matthew were relieved with that news and made a decision to get the fibroid removed. Dinah's mother and sister came down to Houston to be with Dinah during the minor operation.

The operation was scheduled for a Monday and on Saturday night the weekend prior to that Monday, I hosted a big dinner for all of them. We were all laughing and talking and I began clearing the dinner dishes to make way for dessert. Dinah helped me and pulled me aside saying "Gwynn, I had a dream."

"Oh, about the baby coming!" I exclaimed. Dinah said no in a most alarming somber tone.

"Gwynn, I dreamed I didn't make it through the operation," Dinah held my arm and looked into my eyes.

"Oh dear," I sighed, "you are just a bit nervous, everything will be well, I don't want you fret, my love," giving her a big Texas hug. I saw that big smile of hers return and felt relieved that she seemingly calmed down. We continued our tall tales and the evening ended most hilariously, full of laughter and the wonderful energy of close-knit love.

That Monday I reported to work as usual and Dinah's mother phoned me to say Dinah had gone into surgical preparation. I let her know I would come to the hospital on my lunch break. When I arrived at St. Joseph's Hospital, I found Dinah's mom and sisters fearful and anxious. Dinah had not yet come to from the surgery and she should have been awake an hour ago. I told them to sit tight and I would hunt down the surgeon. It took me about 45 minutes to locate him and I finally met him in the cafeteria. He told me the surgery went well and her vital signs were right on target. I informed him that Dinah had not yet come to and her mom and sisters were extremely worried. He said he would find out what doctor administered the initial anesthesia, but when he performed the surgery everything went as expected and it was most successful. We all sat in the lobby that afternoon, all night, and well into the next morning. The nurses and doctors kept running in and out but there was no change in her condition. Around noon, we went home to shower, change clothes. and return to the hospital that afternoon. Still no change and Dinah remained unconscious. I phoned my office and my supervisor the General Manager of Houston Metro and he told me to take whatever time I needed and his prayers were with Dinah and her family. That evening I walked the hospital halls trying to find the surgeon and trying to get the name of the doctor who administered the anesthesia. I began talking to anyone who would talk to me, explaining what had happened to Dinah who had come in for a routine removal of fibroid tumor that was benign so that she could conceive. I was sobbing and had walked the floors of the hospital looking for anyone who would give me the name of the doctor who administered the anesthesia. Hours later, sobbing, I decided to get coffee for Dinah's family, when all of sudden three people pulled me from behind into what I thought was a broom closet. They had grabbed me ever so quickly and before I could scream, the man and two women identified themselves and showed me their hospital badges. The man was a doctor and the two other women were surgical nurses. They said they only had a few minutes to talk to me. They were aware of the person I was looking for. The doctor said Dinah was in a coma and they were not sure if she would ever come out of it. The two nurses stated the doctor who administered the anesthesia was a female. They relayed three other similar situations happening with this same female doctor over the last 30 days where persons she had administered anesthesia to died. No one questioned anything, the doctor stated because all three of those patients were elderly individuals, but now given the fact Dinah was only 26 they suspected some mishap had occurred after the surgeon left. I told them I found the surgeon and he assured me the surgery was successful. I asked them if they could get any other information to me please let me know. Days passed and Dinah remained unconscious and unresponsive and her family and I stayed vigilant in prayer. One night as I went home to shower and

63

to call my son who was with his dad on summer vacation, an incoming call came from my friend in Scottsdale. I ended the call with my son who was excited he and his dad were traveling to Canada. I took the call from my friend Rev. Thomas. I had called her the night before and wanted to tell her what had happened to Dinah. Rev. Thomas was quite a gifted woman who knew Hebrew was able to read and give spiritual guidance to people from all over the world. Many, many famous people benefitted from her gift. I explained to her that Dinah had gone into surgery and everything had seemed okay and that I had spoken to the surgeon who performed the operation and when he left her she was fine. Rev. Thomas told me the female doctor gave her too much anesthesia prior to the surgery. Rev. Thomas said after the surgery was completed she saw Dinah's heart rate going into a risk low level and had given her a dose of another drug attempting to bring the heart rate back to normal. She continued that Dinah was in a coma but more importantly the shock of the overdoses had placed her body in a vegetative state. As I cried uncontrollably over the phone, she informed me Dinah had made a choice to not live in a vegetative state and would move on to her next reincarnation. I shared with Rev. Thomas Dinah's premonition of death through a dream. Rev. Thomas said right now Dinah could hear my voice and to go back to the hospital and pray over her and to hold her hand, and ask her to give me a small sign that she could hear my voice. I hung up, and dressed quickly and drove so fast down Memorial Blvd. that I was pulled over by the Houston police. I explained to the officer why I was speeding to the hospital. He was on a motorcycle and said he would lead me to the hospital through the red lights and to follow him. He led me right to the emergency side of the hospital and said his prayers were with me. I ran into Dinah's room and awakened her mom and sisters. I prayed to God almighty reciting the 23rd psalm as I held Dinah's hand and asked her to give me a small sign that she could hear my voice. We watched, we all watched and they saw Dinah give my hand a squeeze. We all cried and we all told Dinah how much we loved her. In the morning, Dinah passed.

I left Dinah's mother and sisters and began walking the halls in search of the doctor and the two nurses who had pulled me into the broom closet. I found them in the cafeteria and asked them to come outside into the parking lot individually as I did not want anyone to see me speaking with them. They gave me the name of the anesthesiologist after I let them know Dinah had passed earlier that morning.

I went back to work because I had to inform my staff, the General Manager, and hundreds of employees that she had died. Hundreds more filed into my office the remainder of the day. That night I had a class to teach at Texas Southern University. It was a graduate class in the Transportation Center that I was teaching and the night that mid-term papers were due. During the break a small, framed man came over to my room and said you are Gwynn Simpson right? Yes I said. He introduced himself and his last name was the same as the female anesthesiologist. I was shocked, he looked at me in utter silence after that and went back to his classroom. I went to work the next day and explained to my staff what had happened and that I would do everything in God's power to get that doctor disbarred.

The following Saturday was Dinah's memorial service. I was ironing my Jackie Kennedy like suit, it was navy, and I had purchased it a long time ago from the Sakowitz department store before it became a furrier. I dusted off my pillbox hat. When the iron was warm enough, I went to grab the glass of water to put into the iron to make some steam for pressing my navy suit. The glass of water flew off the ironing board into the air. The house began to shake and rattle as though ten Houston like hurricanes were moving through it. I began praying and just pressed the suit as best as I could. I cut my radio onto the gospel station and continued to get ready, amidst what seemed to be the worst crisis of my life. I knelt down beside my bed to pray and the face of the female doctor that I had not yet seen in the flesh appeared. I got up and drove to the memorial service. There were so many, many people, the church was full and the parking lot was full; everyone loved Dinah.

The Curse

That evening when I arrived home, the turmoil increased ten-fold. I remember thinking how glad I was that my son was with his father for the summer and not here to witness this satanic circumstance. I called Rev. Thomas who was in Tucson with some nuns having a meeting. She said Spirit had told her Dinah no longer wanted to live, she would have been in a vegetable state and decided to move on from this lifetime. She strongly encouraged me to call the Trinity Hot-line. I called them and they gave me prayers to say. I prayed all night and all day Sunday and all night Sunday. I called the Trinity Hotline back Monday morning.

I told them how much I had been praying the prayers and I had prayed all day and night and nothing worked. I informed them that everything had escalated beyond belief. The man on the other end of the phone line asked, "Are you the woman from Houston who called before?" I said yes and explained how awful things had become. He paused and said, "You have the greatest prayer warrior in the world right there in Houston. Have you ever heard of John Osteen?" he asked I said yes, I have been to his church in Settegast, TX. Well, he continued, you need to call him to get things settled down. I thanked him and began searching for the number to the church. A little lady answered the phone and I explained to her how I had called the Trinity Hot-line, and how all of these horrific things were happening in my home, how Dinah had died and that the nurses and doctors told me how this anesthesiologist had killed her, and several other people and that I was attempting to get her disbarred and the Trinity Hotline referred me to Rev. John Osteen. She told me to get in the car and come over. I explained it would take me more than an hour to get there. She said, "No worries, we will be here." I got there and found a circle of prayer warriors whose ages if I added up were seemingly more than 1,000 years old. They told me when the curse was broken it would smell something like a dead orchid. I had never smelled a dead orchid and didn't know what to think. They prayed and prayed and then all of a sudden I did smell something awfully peculiar. "It is done," they informed me and after blessing me sent me on my way. I drove home thinking what kind of life have I had, what extraordinary experiences have I gone through. I kept wondering was I just plain abnormal or were similar things happening to people all over the world like this? I began talking to God and asking him to tell me in plain language what my mission was as a single mom, 44 years old with an 11-year-old son in tow. I promised myself to keep my head on and my feet firmly planted on the ground for surely God did not want me to crack up over this incident. Yet oddly enough, I did not feel frightened, I felt energized even though noon had passed and I had nothing at all to eat that day. I was glad that I had taken off from work, as I did not have the mindset to do any work. When I arrived home there was nothing but peace. There was no noise like the winds of a hurricane; no cracking in the walls like someone was tearing down my townhome, no eerie lights, and no glasses of water flying up in the ceiling. The energy was indescribable and I thought surely those ancient prayer warriors had blessed this crazy Creole. I also began to think why it is that they accepted me and told me to come? Were they familiar with curses? Did they understand voodoo or was it that they understood evil and that it had no power against the faithful. I had heard of people who visit folks practicing black magic but had never been a victim of it. My mother, grandmother, great-grandmother, my Aunt Mimi, and sister Dorsey had all reminded me to stay prayed up because people like us who have a 6th sense might be subjected to an attack. When I was a young girl, I always thought what kind of attack are they talking about, but as I grew older I learned what they meant; a spiritual attack by someone evil. That doctor had killed several older people in the hospital whose relatives did not question their passing. Dinah was too young to die, she had a future with a new husband and her daughter. She was loved by everyone who met her and was the brightest of lights to many employees within our organization. How is it that such a horrible deed ended her life so soon? Was it Karma or the transference of negative energy?

The next week I had another minister come to bless my home and it remained in peace for the six years I lived there until another position relocated me to the east coast. At every opportunity, while in Houston I went to hear Rev. Osteen. Though I have never been to the Compact Center to hear his son, I have read a number of Joel Osteen's books and I tape his televised sermons every Sunday. I live by them because these sermons set the tone for every week in my life. I have encouraged all of my friends of every faith to tune in, as his messages are truly heavenly and relate to a higher consciousness for living. His messages are my invisible stars of positivity that provide me light in all of my relationships. I will forever be thankful for those prayer warriors who brought everlasting peace into my spirit.

That doctor had gone to New Orleans and put a curse on me. Through God, I put a curse on her career and got her dismissed. I look back at those events and I still question how it is that those events popped up into my life? Was this my Karma? Was it Dinah's Karma? Was this a karmic lesson I had to learn in order to be knowledgeable about the true power of the Lord? Was it a lesson given to me so that I could write this book to let others know that the people we meet all have a meaning and purpose in our lives? Was it a karmic lesson to instruct me on the power of the transference of negative energy and how destructive negative energy can be in the hands of evil people? I had grown up hearing about people in New Orleans who practiced "voodoo" but was always taught that God is the "Author and the Finisher" and evil under no circumstances will triumph the power of God the Almighty. I think of Dinah often, her picture stands tall with the pictures of my family. Dinah was family and I feel blessed to have met her in this lifetime. However, voodoo is alive and well. I recently returned from a conference where I became aware one of the speakers has published a book on such practices that conjure up spirits. I had been told by family of the dark side of this so-called religion and now, having lived through the results of the experience with Dinah, I know the true power of meditation, prayer, and walking in the light.

Chapter Ten
Mind-Speak

Our Internal Self-Talk

We Are Who We Think We Are?

Our thoughts make up our internal highway of mind-speak and our mind-speak often becomes the road map for future roots of action.

Speaking of highways, one day I was driving down a busy six-lane freeway thinking of how hurt I was from a relationship with a man. I began to think of some of horrible incidents that should occur to him to pay him back for all of my hurt and all of the other women he had trespassed. All of a sudden, a huge 18-wheeler tire, being hauled with a bunch of other 18-wheeler tires on a truck across the six-lane freeway going in the opposite direction of me in my jeep, bounced off into the air, hopped over the freeway, and crashed into my windshield and the hood of my jeep. I panicked and someone (a guardian angel) steered my jeep toward the space between the lane and guardrail lane. Two teenagers in a car behind me called the police and pulled up behind me to see if I was alive. They waited with me and showed the highway patrolman a picture of the tire jumping in the air across the freeway that they captured on their cell phone. They waited until the tow truck came for my jeep and they gave me a ride home. They were tattooed from the tip of their noses to the bottom of their feet yet they were kind, compassionate, intelligent, and giving. The police phoned in and another highway patrolman caught the truck, got the license and insurance information. Later that night the policeman came to check on me and provided me with the insurance information.

While I repaired my jeep, I began working on repairing my negative thoughts and mind-speak about this person. I thanked my guardian angel for saving me and pleaded for forgiveness. I thought, *Oh my, another piece of my horrible behavior is being entered into the Akashic Record.* I wondered how much more grief would my mental insanity cause me in this lifetime. Needless to say, that evening I returned to prayer and meditation and severely curtailed any thoughts of him. When a thought of him occasionally slipped into my consciousness, I said a prayer for him, envisioned the Christ light around him, and wished him well.

Honest Conversations

Sometimes we get a wake-up call in the strangest forms. It shakes us up and makes us re-think our negative behaviors. We must begin to take caution to have honest conversations with ourselves about our self-talk, and our mind-speak. In viewing a hurt, we must begin to dissect it like we did in biology in high school. Pinpointing in our minds why that hurt is still there and questioning our ego to discover why we are allowing the hurt to continue to control our emotional wellbeing. This is a must mental exercise we have to practice when we allow negative thoughts to fester. We have to examine our current environment to see what triggers or surfaces that old hurt into our present day consciousness? Ask what does that old hurt prevent me from doing? Has that old hurt taken away a body part? Does that old hurt prevent me from performing on my job? Does that old hurt prevent me from being a good parent? Does that old hurt interfere with any of my daily habits or prevent me from having friends or being a friend to others? Does that old hurt prevent me from driving, traveling, eating, or enjoying the company of others? Is that old hurt interfering with any of my present-day relationships? Does that old hurt prevent me from having sex, trying on a new piece of clothing, going to a concert, sporting event, church, or family outing? Is that old hurt controlling my mind-speak? Do I bring up that old hurt in any conversation about relationships with people?

Then ask yourself who is in control, you, or the hurt? If you answer the hurt, go see a mental health professional.

Otherwise question even further why you are giving such a great amount of energy to the hurt, to the extent that you are allowing the hurt to control you?

Finally answer the question for yourself of what value is it to give such control to an event of the past? Ask yourself what are you getting in return from hanging onto a previous hurt, especially when the person who hurt you has moved on? **Remind yourself that your retention**

of the hurt in your "mind-speak," and "self-talk" is by no means hurting the person who hurt you!

Mindset is a most powerful tool. It can be quite useful when targeted towards a positive goal.

A Choice

When I graduated from high school, Daddy asked me if I wanted to be a Debutante like my sister. That was part of that old "southern culture"; purportedly as young lady you had to be presented to "society." Growing up in Houston, society was beer, barbeque, the YWCA, mass, bazaars, girl scouts, and my summer trips to New Orleans. I could not conceive in my mind of what value would it be to spend money on a gown that resembled a wedding dress and marching through a path of rose petals would have for my future. We lived in a fairly segregated community and the people hosting these "coming out" and "presenting to society events" were the same old folks I saw every day in the beauty shop and at the corner grocery store. I could not understand how such an event of nonsense on one night would change my entire being. They made much ado about these nights, fathers dancing with their daughters and giving the evil eye to the young men who escorted them. Aside from that, the cost for such an event was ridiculous and wasteful. I was reminded of the partying Marie Antoinette in France who enjoyed many a night as the French Revolution came to rip out her heart. With no sense of the poor and destitute and disregard for their oppressed status was reflected in her most insidious statement of "let them eat cake" forever follows her in recorded history. Daddy, being an equalitarian, thought he would ask because my sister had chosen that route, but in his heart I believe he knew I would never follow her path.

I had my mind set on something bigger, something grander, something much more phenomenal than a one-night debutante stand. Spirit told me I would have a chance to see the world and I chose a college based on three factors; 2000 miles away from Houston, a Catholic college, and one that offered study abroad. My parents insisted I attend a catholic college, not my choice, but a mandate. I wanted to go to UCLA or USC. I wanted to make sure the college was at least 2,000 miles away from Houston, that way Daddy could not come up and check on me during the weekends. But most important was the fact that the college I chose St. Thomas Aquinas in Grand Rapids, Michigan, offered the Study Abroad Program typically for Junior-class students. Little did they know that this Creole country girl from Houston, TX, had made up her mind to attend this college based solely on that offering? Mindset is a powerful thing and during the first part of my freshman year when they began announcing it for the following year, I determined I was going. I completed the paperwork and after that, all I had to do was to go home for Christmas and convince my dad to pay for it.

Chapter Eleven
Rebirth

Could These Be Possible Trajectories of Famous People?

Believe It or Not

Was Oprah, a billionaire in this lifetime, and an entrepreneurial millionaire in the last one living as the famous Madame C. J. Walker, the first female African-American millionaire? Did Prince Harry abdicate the throne in his previous lifetime as he married the twice divorcee, Wallis Simpson, and now in his current existence having dated women of all races married Megan Markle in 2018 who recently gave birth to their son, Archie. Meghan Markle, a divorcee and star of "Suits" has impacted the world's perception of who can be royal? Steve Jobs may have turned on quite a different light bulb in the 21st century having developed an instrument that would remove the darkness of communication, enlightening the world with computerized communication. Could his interest in bringing light to our world have stemmed from a previous lifetime as Thomas Edison? It is worthwhile to explore the similarities in some of the 21st century's most impactful people.

There is no one on our planet like Oprah Winfrey. There are not enough words in any language to describe the impact she has had on millions of people from around the globe. She continues to instruct us on how to be "human," bringing to the surface topics hidden from the dinner tables because of their emotional shadows. Oprah brought the concept of televised self-help to the masses. We related to her because of her ability to turn personality traits inside out and upside down, teaching us how to move away from the shame of our ego-controlled behavioral habits into the "spiritual light" of purpose for ourselves. There exist no one like her and I dare say there will be few in the future who can create the pathways of health and emotional wellness that she has imprinted in modern history.

Madam C.J. Walker

If indeed there are no coincidences or accidents within our universe than surely the fact that the original intended name of Orpah did not stick, was not a mistake of the universe. Legends are often characterized by their actions and deeds. Orpah, known as OPRAH to the rest of world, "is breeding love" to everyone on our planet. Our lives change when we choose spiritual energy over the illusion of the physical environment.

Let's take a look at two women born in two distinct eras, and distinct states, who rose from the depths of impoverishment into skies of remarkable accomplishments. In spite of the challenges emerging through their birth environments, both were uniquely gifted with persistence and an understanding of how to bring dreams to fruition. Both were born southern black women and both became successful financial entrepreneurs, learning to take advantage of the formidable odds against them. By helping others succeed they both became legendary.

Madame C. J. Walker, as she later became known in the pages of history, was born Sarah Breedlove on December 23, 1867, in Delta, Louisiana, to emancipated free slaves. Madame C. J. Walker became the first female black millionaire in the United States. Eighty-seven years later and less than 116 miles from Sarah's birthplace, Orpah, later to be known as Oprah, was born January 29, 1954, in Kosciusko, Mississippi, and eventually emerged as America's first female black billionaire.

They appeared to have shared some early common circumstances in their rise toward notoriety. Both women had been born in significant poverty and experienced significant changes at their tender ages of six. Oprah who spent her youngest years with a grandmother that taught her to read at the age of three moved to Milwaukee when she was six. Sarah Breedlove, whose parents died when she was six years old, was sent to live with her sister, Louvinia, in Vicksburgh, Mississippi. Unable to either read or write, Sarah worked as a housemaid there with her sister.

At the age of 14, both women experienced unique life-changing experiences. Sarah found herself in an abusive environment living in the home of her sister and brother-in-law and chose to marry at the age of fourteen to escape it. Oprah on the other hand was abused and molested by several family members and at the age of 14 became pregnant with a son who later died shortly after birth.

Sarah, now married and having moved to St. Louis gave birth to a daughter, Leila, and was 20 when her first husband died. She worked very hard for the next 18 years as a laundress.

Like Oprah during the course of her lifetime, Madame C. J. Walker found herself engaged in several relationships. She married two other gentlemen, the last of which she divorced but later adopted his initials and used his last name becoming Madame C. J. Walker. Prior to this union, Sarah Breedlove, now Walker, educated her daughter, became a member of African Methodist Church, sang in the choir, and began a process of self-education.

Oprah Winfrey traveled a different course and after the pregnancy, her mother returned her to her father, Vernon Winfrey. At the age of 17, Oprah moved to Nashville, Tennessee, and began living with him. Albeit he was strict, Oprah thrived in high school and attained a scholarship to Tennessee State University. Her debate and oratory skills earned her an opportunity with a radio station while still in high school and at the age of 19 began co-anchoring the news. At 19, Oprah had become the first African-American TV correspondent and the youngest person to co-anchor the news for WTVF television. Over her next 18 years, Oprah syndicated The Oprah Winfrey Show, created HARPO Productions, and starred in a TV mini-series, *The Women of Brewster Place*.

Oprah is a known proponent of clean eating, proper nutrition, and exercise, and has encouraged individuals all over the world to make good and meaningful changes in their diet and behavioral health. Early in her career, she disclosed at one point in her life she lost her hair due to a bad perm. Sarah faced a similar challenge with the application of harsh products such as lye included in soap products for cleansing hair. Similar to Oprah, Sarah lost her hair and it was this loss that became the impetus for her discovery of hair care products safe for use by black women. She invented products to help re-grow her own hair. Sarah, like Oprah, showed great concern for the health of black people who at the time suffered from poor nutrition, illness, and the proper care of washing hair at a time when few black people had indoor plumbing, or electricity for central heating.

Sarah's calling to provide better health care products for black women led her into door to door sales of products, the establishment of a beauty college named after her daughter Leila, the commission of more than 3,000 employees and the construction of a factory in Indianapolis to produce her health and beauty product lines.

Sarah's lifelong mission of providing the best information in health and beauty aids for black hair was surpassed only by Oprah's zeal to televise to her worldwide audiences the latest advancements in physical health and nutrition as well as emotional and spiritual wellbeing for us living in the new millennium.

Madame C. J. Walker, aka Sarah Breedlove, like Oprah, became a successful activist and philanthropist. Madame C. J. Walker gave bonuses to outstanding salespersons and also rewarded those who made the largest contributions to charities in their communities.

Oprah's list of philanthropic efforts are too numerous to list yet everyone will recall the large and meaningful gifts awarded to members of the audiences during her TV Talk Shows. Oprah's spirit is one of love and charity with respect for all of humanity. Sarah bred love through the United States, the Caribbean, and Latin America with entrepreneurial activities focused on women, children, and people of African descent. Oprah's love continues to ignite a planetary people of all races, sexual orientations, philosophies, religions, varied social statues, and beliefs. Known for building schools in Africa for young girls and creating the television network, OWN, to promote the health and psychological wellbeing of women, Oprah has impacted the health and spirituality of millions of people throughout the world.

Could it be that one carries the accomplishments, the wishes, and the hopes from one lifetime into another incarnation? Could it be that the unfinished mission of Madame C. J. Walker, whose life ended prematurely at the age of 51 blossomed and enlarged in another lifetime through America's first female black billionaire, Oprah Gail Winfrey? Can it be said that our beautiful and spirited Oprah took the Karma from a previous lifetime as Madame C. J. Walker and entered into this lifetime continuing to make our world all the better through her divine, intelligent spirit?

Oprah has just won the Cecil B. DeMille Award for 2018 and in what few critics claimed to be a political acceptance, Oprah once again spoke of our planet as one, and the right of everyone including females to be part of its ongoing history in a way that excludes harassment. There is talk from those who wish her to run for the President of the United States, yet in her own right, Oprah is far beyond America and is all "ah staged" for the world!

England's Prince

Watching him follow behind the coffin of the "World's Princess," who just happened to be his mother, is still a daunting thought lying in the remembrances of many people's minds and hearts. What courage the young do have in trembling circumstances? A devoted and loving mother Diana's life was snipped as a fresh garden rose lying in the height of its bloom. The world visibly mourned as it had for no other person in history. The funeral of Diana was watched in every country by millions who felt they knew her because their hearts had been touched by her loving actions for all people from every dominion. The world cried tears it did not know it had for someone who changed completely the consciousness of the earth itself.

Henry Charles Albert David; Prince Henry of Wales, born September 15, 1984, was just shy of his 13th birthday when he took the long walk that would plunge him into a different reality with the death of his mother; "The People's Princess."

There continues to be the controversy over whether or not Prince Charles is Prince Harry's father? It should be noted people often take on the physical traits of a previous lifetime and if indeed reincarnation is a true fact, perhaps Prince Harry's red hair comes from the previous incarnation of Edward VIII or the person we have come to know as the

Duke of Windsor upon his marriage to twice divorcee, Wallis Simpson.

Edward VIII shared the same voracity of life as Prince Harry; the military, sports, and women. He crossed the lines of bureaucracy and ultimately was led by his heart. A heart that would dethrone his future as a king. The ruddiness, the reddish hair, the seriousness of self can be seen between the two men. The independence of spirit transferred from one incarnation into the other, however Prince Harry's educational and humanitarian explorations in this short time period have taken him farther to shores unexperienced by Edward VIII in his lifetime.

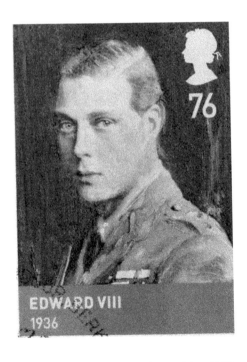

The picture above shows quite a bit of likeness and Prince Edward VIII, named Prince of Wales at 16, later to become the Duke of Windsor, had the brilliant reddish hair similar to Prince Harry. Like Prince Harry, Prince Edward VIII was wildly enthusiastic about sports and was extremely instrumental in the erection of Wembley Stadium for the British Empire Exhibition. Prince Harry created importance for the Invictus Games, Para-Olympic competition honoring war veterans. They both earned their pilots license and served in the British Armed Services.

Prince Edward was a prolific romantic and perhaps his father gave him the lease of Fort Belvedere to smother the fire of his relationships with several married women, one of whom would eventually lead him to Wallis Simpson.

It was rumored Prince Edward VIII was a Nazi sympathizer, and most will recall Prince Harry's brush with the same anathema when he adorned a Halloween costume with a Nazi relic, for which he later apologized.

Unlike Edward VIII, Prince Harry has dated women of all nationalities and colors. His wife, Megan Markle, like Wallis Simpson was a divorcee. His wife, Megan, is indeed a divorcee like Wallis Simpson and is of mixed race—African-American and Anglo—and starred on a televised drama, "Suits." The Queen has welcomed Markle into the Royal Family and has given them the Cottage of Frogmore to make their home.

While Meghan Markle is no Wallis Simpson, she is uncommonly out of the traditional royal box, an independent spirit, unafraid of the rules, regulations, and expectations for members of British Royalty. The Queen stated in her Christmas message of 2017 that she looked forward to welcoming new members into her family, sending to everyone her blessing of Prince Harry's choice.

The American media anchor, Brian Williams characterized this engagement well, "two people, simply in love," and this is just a mere reflection of the Prince's mother Diana, who walked with people from every designated caste system and every societal label to teach us that love has no color. It is beautiful to see just two people in love walking together, knowing love is beyond color, race, religion and all of the other socio-philosophical titles society has tried to attach to unconditional love. This royal union is a lesson to the world that love is light and Prince Harry's incarnation in these modern times will move many souls into enlightenment.

Two Titans in Different Worlds of Light

Both were born in February and both died in October. Both considered great entrepreneurs, one of the Industrial Age and the other in the era of Modern Technology. Thomas Alva Edison born February 11, 1847 and Steve Jobs born February 24, 1955 were considered self-educated men, neither one attaining a formal college degree.

They were two inventors and two businessmen who preferred their work to their families. Edison literally brought physical light to the world through the incandescent light bulb and Jobs ushered in the light of instant mobile communications. Edison suffered a hearing loss at an early age and Jobs suffered a hearing loss of other people's opinions. Both were driven toward perfection and both felt they were the only ones who could define what that meant in terms of their trade. Both were fired at significant points in their lives. Edison early on from his telegraph job with the associated press from spilling sulfuric acid, and Jobs for spilling the anguish of his determination upon those he considered office minions attempting to serve him.

While Edison is attributed to inventing the movie camera for motion pictures, Jobs, if indeed the reincarnation of Edison, developed technology for animated motion pictures produced by Pixar. Edison earlier significantly impacted global communication with the development of the first carbon transmitter for the telephone. Jobs took the telephone one step further, making it mobile and ushering in the mass production of cell phones that expedited mass communications around the world. Edison developed the phonograph and Jobs created a singular device that could message, email, accept calls from a telephonic cell device; play music and movies, navigate roadways whether walking or driving and access the universal keeper of electronic information, the almighty internet.

In the photo above, Edison resembles a young Steve Jobs with dark hair and a distinct air of confidence. Like Jobs, Edison's inventions were the result of his numerous collaborations with engineers. Edison's death was the result of complications with diabetes, and Jobs from pancreatic cancer. It is now believed that the onset of diabetes in people over 50 maybe a precursor to pancreatic cancer, as both diseases reveal difficulty in producing insulin. Both Edison and Jobs conducted lifelong work evolving around virtually the same thing, "transmitters" in various forms transmitting surrounded the base technology of all of their inventions.

Clearly Good-Looking and Cool

Clark Gable starred in more than 60 films during his lifetime; raised a Roman Catholic, Clark was born William Clark Gable on February 1, 1901 and died at the age of 59 on November 16, 1960. Clark Gable greatly resembles another well know actor George Timothy Clooney and within their given names share two prominent letters of G and C interchangeably in their first and last names.

In these names Clark Gable and George Clooney, we notice similar alphabetical letters such as the R, E, L, and I. Gable may have reincarnated as George Clooney on May 6, 1961.

What is striking are the uncommonly good looks and amazing acting abilities of both men. The eyes, eyebrows, cheekbones, and facial construction of both men are strikingly comparable. Gable born to a protestant father and Roman Catholic mother was baptized in the Catholic Church, as was George. Gable and Clooney both had astonishing relationships with women. Carol Lombard reportedly was the love of Gable's life and surely the beautiful, poised, and prominently well-educated Amal Alamuddin has the heart and soul of Clooney.

Clooney's notoriety popularized through the long-running television series ER, he starred in 28 films from 1996 and 2016. Clooney won an Oscar for Best Supporting Actor in Syriana and has been nominated for six academy awards in different categories. Gable was nominated three times; "Mutiny on the Bounty," "Gone with the Wind," and "It happened One Night" won an Oscar for Best Actor.

Both Gable and Clooney are considered "debonair" in the sheerest sense of the word; well-dressed and great communicators with unforgettable prescience.

Clooney in this short lifetime has brought a consciousness of humanitarian need in under-developed countries, some of which continue to be in the throes of tribal wars. He has made strident steps in creating charitable organizations and fighting for charitable causes. His sense of the right of freedom for human health and social welfare equity cuts across all cultural lines. Both Gable and Clooney had children in their '50s. It was rumored that Gable had a child, a girl with Loretta Young, which was never acknowledged until the death of Judy Young. Gable later had a child with his fourth wife, a boy.

Clooney recently had twins with his second wife, Amal Alamuddin. Without the mustache, there is a striking resemblance of who Clooney may have been in a previous lifetime.

George Timothy Clooney has been a United Nations Messenger of peace since 2008 and has awakened people all over our earth to the tragedies of 9/11, Darfur, Armenian Genocide, 2004 Tsunami, and the 2010 Haiti earthquake. He did not condition his efforts on the false belief that individuals from oppressed countries are subterranean human beings. He has taken a road of higher consciousness in bringing relief to problems of starvation, lack of clean water systems, and healthcare for babies and children who are victims from war. He has not characterized people in communities who lack the industrialized tools to promote agriculture as sub-human. He has not scorned individuals who are in need of a hand-up. No George Timothy Clooney has raised millions upon millions of dollars in an effort to bring humanitarian equity to people suffering regardless of tribal belief, regardless of skin color, regardless of caste and status. Clooney's outreach to the world has been of a higher calling and his generosity can be seen in the kindness of his tongue. He has made our world better and without a doubt his name like other earth angels will find its way into "the good book."

Sluggers

The New York Yankees maintain a historical reputation of getting the best and being the best. Their diehard, forever fans span generations and they wear their badges of honor in all ways fathomable. Yankee fans are boastful and more often than not, Yankee players over the years have given to the game of baseball an equivalency of Star Wars excitement!

Reportedly, George Herman Ruth, later to evolve as the "babe" of baseball, hit the longest home run in history. At the age of seven, he was sent to St. Mary's Industrial School for Boys, where his family rarely visited him, and where five years later he was allowed to attend his mother's funeral. Babe played street ball and busted quite a few windows and some believe that to be the primary reason the youth perceived as incorrigible by his family was sent away.

Ruth played 22 seasons with the New York Yankees and Jeter's incredible career spanning 19 years witnessed his #2 Jersey being retired on May 14, 2017. Babe Ruth died before his #3 Jersey was retired, however the baseball commissioner appointed April 27, 1947 "Babe Ruth Day" a year later after a diagnosis in 1946 of a malignant tumor at the base of his skull. More than 60,000 people witnessed the tribute to Ruth in the "House that Ruth Built."

Jeter's childhood was considered normal with an Irish/German mother and an African-American father who held a Ph.D. Jeter graduated high school in Kalamazoo, Michigan. Ruth's father owned a saloon in Baltimore and housed the family in an apartment above. After an incident in the saloon, the city authorities declared the environment unfit for a child and sent the young "Babe" to St. Mary's Reformatory School. His parents were German, yet Ruth suffered from derogatory and offensive behaviors from other boys who felt Ruth did not look like a typical German. Though Ruth spoke German as a youth, his facial features and lips resembled a person of African-American descent. I refuse to publish the racial nicknames attributed to Ruth by hagglers. However, Ruth became known as "the Babe," "the

Bambino," and "the Sultan of Swat." Jeter born in a more respectful era of diversity became known as "Mr. Clutch" and "Mr. November" for his heroism on the field.

Ruth, albeit married for the bulk of his life, was a known womanizer and many felt it cost him a management job after retiring from the major leagues. He purportedly stated he could slow down on his beer drinking and get to bed earlier at night but would not give up women because they were fun. Married as a teenager to his first wife, Helen Woodford, who died at age 31 and who separated from Ruth a few years before her death because of his numerous infidelities. In a biography, the daughter he and the first wife Helen adopted was actually his biological daughter from his relationship with a mistress, Juanita Jennings.

Jeter, similar to Ruth is an enormous personality. Prolific in his craft as a baseball player, Jeter has been in and out of high profile relationships with celebrities. Ruth may have out bat Jeter in the womanizing department, however, it is worth noting that Jeter dated intelligent, beautiful, and purposeful women. The majority of those he dated were considered A-Listers in the crafts of acting, modeling, music, directing, and producing. While many of these relationships were publicized through social media, Jeter maintained the respect of both his fans and fellow players. Like Ruth, he was counted on in clutch situations especially in November during the World Series.

A product of a bi-racial marriage, his parents made him sign contracts to ensure good behavior. And it paid off as Jeter, in this lifetime, handled himself respectfully coupled with a huge sense of humility. He displayed a likeable public persona and people around the world loved him for being down to earth and respecting the industry that afforded him fame.

While Ruth was penalized for his past relationships, if he is indeed Derek Jeter in this lifetime, he will be able to claim any management position that baseball has to offer.

Unlike Ruth, Jeter was unmarried as he, like many young high profile men dated several women of great substance, which in the final analysis points to perhaps lessons well learned from the past and reflects the caliber of his character in modern times.

A lovely young woman, Hanna Davis, became Mrs. Jeter in 2016 and on August 17, 2017, Derek Jeter became father to Bella Raine Jeter.

Like Babe Ruth, Jeter today is one of baseball's most celebrated players and surely his enormous accomplishments on and off the field will result in his induction into the "Hall of Fame."

The Content of Character

Still debated in America today, we continue to question how and why and for what reason do we continue to ignore the "content of character" in our discussions on the issue of race.

David Walker wrote "An Appeal to the Colored Citizens of the World," asking slaves and all colored people to unite against the oppression of white slave owners in America. This pamphlet proved to be a discourse on the inequities and inhuman actions taken against slaves by white Americans. His words fought so strongly against racial inequalities that even Abolitionists felt him to be too radical for the times.

Walker characterized slave owners as pretenders to Christianity. He likened their treatment of slaves to that of the Pharaoh of Egypt against the Israelites. Walker brought to light the cheapness of slavery and how the no-cost labor played to the avariciousness of slave masters who chose to ignore the inhumanity of treating human beings less than animal chattel.

He informed readers of the God of the Heavens who would one day give an ear to the cries of the oppressed and who would appear on their behalf to destroy the oppressors. He reminded slave owners that God works in mysterious ways, of his wonders to perform, and cited historical uprisings from the Egyptians being hurled into the Red Sea; the murder of Caesar and the final annihilation of Constantinople. He stated that white Americans who call themselves enlightened and Christian people have treated their slaves worse than any other nation. By inculcating into their belief systems that slaves enjoyed their destitute conditions, white Americans were able to turn deaf ears and eyes to the wretched conditions they imposed upon the enslaved. In one line of his pamphlet, Walker cited the example of Pharaoh giving Joseph an Egyptian wife and retorted that marrying a white woman was not worth a pinch of snuff, which he would never consider giving for such a marriage.

Similar to Dr. Martin Luther King, David Walker had a strong church affiliation and maintained close ties with the African Methodist Episcopal Church during his lifetime. Like Dr. King, his lifespan was short and Walker died at the age of 33 on August 6, 1830. We have no picture for David Walker but we have his intent, purpose, and written word to compare to the unfinished business he left in his lifetime that I believe Dr. King assumed in this incarnation. We know David Walker had a head full of hair, average height, and like King withstood the weight of angry racial times.

Close to a century later came a modern day freedom fighter whose oral and written capabilities fueled a nation to remove from law the inability of "the colored man and woman" to be free in America. Dr. Martin Luther King, Pastor of Dexter Avenue Baptist Church was born on January 15, 1929 and named Michael King. He rose to prominence through self-sacrifice, immense faith, and an ability to see beyond the five senses and more importantly because of his defense of a woman named Rosa.

King's name was changed to Martin Luther King Jr. after a trip his father made to Berlin, Germany for a Baptist Conference, where he got the idea to change their names in honor of the German reformer, Martin Luther.

As a child he began to earn a little notoriety for his singing and he later joined the church's junior choir. But his true gift would emerge in high school where he began to perfect the artistry of debate and oratory. He paid close attention to the examples of racism pointed out by his father and was sensitive to offensive behaviors of segregationists and Jim Crow Laws upon non-whites, specifically in the South. The young King was a quick study and passed the entrance exams to Morehouse College at the age of 15 as a junior in high school. King graduated from Morehouse and entered Crozer Theological Seminary in Pennsylvania and later obtained a Ph.D. from Boston University.

Unlike in his perhaps his previous lifetime as David Walker, who would not "give a pinch of snuff to marry a white woman," King fell in love with a German girl whose mother worked in the cafeteria of Morehouse College. His friends were dead set against the friendship. After his mother's disparagement over the idea of engagement and marriage to her, King ended the relationship over the following six months.

King was 24 when he married Coretta Scott, 26 on the lawn of her parents' home in Alabama. National attention arrived when Rosa Parks refused to relinquish her seat to a white bus rider and King's actions wrote pages of history by initiating the 385 day Montgomery Bus Boycott. His home was subsequently bombed and he was arrested. While

Walker emerged as a threat to white Americans, Dr. King Jr. was viewed as a nuclear bomb aimed at white privilege.

His presence in this lifetime played out on an international stage.

Tensions heated up in the South between blacks and whites, and Dr. King did not veer away from the non-violent strategy in spite of the fiery rhetoric of Black adversaries such as Malcolm X, Stokely Carmichael, and Omali Yeshitela.

In 1957, he, Ralph Abernathy, and others formed the Southern Christian Leadership Council (SCLC). When the evangelist Bill Graham befriended Dr. King and his first key public speech "Prayers to Pilgrims for Freedom" was made, a white credibility platform of Christian leaders formed underneath SCLC.

The following year during the signing of his book, "Stride Towards Freedom," a deranged black woman, Izola Curry, stabbed him, forcing surgery, and an extended hospital stay. King would not be silenced and his voice through the written word came through his sermons, "What Is Man" and the publication of "The Meaning of Man." Woven throughout the sermons, public speeches, and publications were the ideas of God's love, God's mercy, and God's grace as well as criticism of segregationists, "Jim Crow Laws," and people behaviors consistent with racial injustice.

King became dismayed with Washington political leadership and although he attended a White House meeting in June of 1963, he continued as David Walker had done to dispel the myth that one could be both Christian and racist. King felt President Kennedy should have been much more expedient in following the footsteps of President Lincoln, enacting a second Emancipation Proclamation prescribing civil and human rights for colored people in America.

The fallout from the larger-scaled Civil Rights movement resurfaced the mood and fears experienced by blacks and whites in David Walker's era. The continued descriptions of inhumanities as well as the televised pictures of the persecution of blacks heightened the apprehension of whites about what life would look like if blacks attained legislative freedom. Herbert Hoover's trepidation of the sheer magnitude and force of the Civil Rights Movement led to his directing President Kennedy to approve the wiretapping of King's phone under the pretense that SCLC was influenced by communism. It was believed that when the organization of the Great March on Washington was taking place, President Kennedy worried over the numbers of those who would actually turn out on the Washington Mall.

Little did JFK know that the strong network of black community churches would support and fund the March. Those who could not attend were instructed to meet in groups to watch the event televised. In our community of Third Ward in Houston, all of the girls I attended school with met at the YWCA to view the March on Washington. We were dressed in our "Sunday Go to Meeting Best" and we represented all economic stratus from the projects to those whose parents were considered professional. We met in solidarity and knew that our futures depended upon Dr. King's ability to change the mindsets of the oppressors. We sat awestruck as Dr. King delivered his most powerful speech ever; one that showed the world he was anointed by

God and his charisma was preparing the necessary pathway for black freedom.

After the unthinkable happened, the assassination of President John Fitzgerald Kennedy, Lyndon Baines Johnson assumed responsibility for getting the Civil Rights Legislation passed by any means necessary. The memory of the more than 250,000 people attending the March of Washington on August 28, 1963 was still vivid in the minds of the entire nation. Bob Dylan and Joan Baez sang "When the Ship Comes In" and "Only a Pawn in Their Game" showing black people that enlightened whites stood as stakeholders with them and supported a unification of all people replete with human rights. The powerful Gospel singer Mahalia Jackson defined the moment of the March on Washington with a rendition of "How I Got Over."

The March on Washington was Dr. King's profound national moment, where a glimmer of light from a long tunnel dug by many Abolitionists revealed the radical writings of David Walker. With no formal education, Walker's persistence and landmark pamphlet was a wake-up call for both whites and black. Coming into a new lifetime if reincarnated as Dr. Martin Luther King, he achieved the legislation he longed for to free black people.

Dr. King has no civil rights equal in modern history. He internationalized the philosophy of civil and human rights. He received the Nobel Prize for Peace and he peacefully closed a segment of the 400-year gap in black history. The breadth of his impact goes unmeasured yet the unification of his beliefs for equality in race, sex, religion, and sexual preference shepherded an unmatched respect for every aspect of acceptable behavior in our world's society.

Light Beings Are Human Beings

If we come back, if we reincarnate into other lifetimes, does not our purpose remain the same, to be of service to one another, to respect one another, and to love one another. These principles of spirituality have not changed since the time of Adonai, Moses, Buddha, Jesus; in Hebrew referred to as (Yeshua), St. Peter, Mohammed, Martin Luther or any other historical prophet or saint. We are commanded by a Creator, whatever you call Him or however you refer to him to uphold and respect all of humanity.

Scientists have informed us of the changing of the earth's rotation. It has sped up and the speed of the earth impacts our body's magnetic field. We have been told we are what we eat and we are what we think and we are how we act. With the increase of the speed of the earth and the impact of how we live in and on planet earth, natural disasters appear to be on the rise. We are a politically divided nation and America still suffers from different perspectives on color, race, religion, sexual orientation, philosophy, and national origin. The media reinforces images of youthful human likenesses in an aging society where many of those images are unachievable for the great masses. We are a society who looks outside of ourselves toward material acquisition in an effort to feel whole in a world based upon vanity and glamour.

Unsurpassed levels of depression, suicide, mass murder, and large economic struggles plague our varied populations. Poverty levels have increased as our inability to provide basic food, clothing, shelter, and education for our families and extended families has increased. Millions of children go un-adopted and animals and pets die of starvation daily.

We continue to label ourselves as human beings, yet our struggle for power in a world that feeds upon war makes us inhuman. We are unable to fully support the impoverishment of other nations impacted by power, greed, and a lack of technology. We are judgmental and we evaluate other cultures unlike ourselves in behavior and thinking. We adopt attitudes of intolerance and seek to control many who shun our way of life where money is a God and sex is a religion. We label them in categories of "less than," and this evil creates the lack of clean water and food that further contributes to impoverishment and death throughout our planet. Though charity abounds the impact of it, around the world falls short. We fall prey to wants rather than needs. We fall prey to the "glamors" of the world; external materialism, greed, sexual abusiveness, and "I-Me-My-Selfish behaviors." We are caught up in a cycle of self that disavows the very principles of spiritual people.

WE CAN CHANGE, IF WE KNOW, WE DO COME BACK TO UNFINISHED BUSINESS.

References

1. Edgar Cayce, www.edgarcayce.org
As accessed on November 19, 2017

2. Edgar Cayce, www.edgarcayce.org
As accessed on November 19, 2017

3. Ryan, Thomas. "Reincarnation After Death," October 21, 2015, in www.AmericanMagazine.com
As accessed on November 19, 2017

4. Semkiw, Walter, M.D., "Reincarnation, Kabala, Judaism, Essenes, Pharisees," from the book Born Again and the Return of the Revolutionaries, 2003, as found on www.Iisis.org
As accessed on November 19, 2017

5. Semkiw, Walter, M.D., "Reincarnation, Kabala, Judaism, Essenes, Pharisees," from the book Born Again and the Return of the Revolutionaries, 2003 as found on www.Iisis.org
As accessed on November 19, 2017

6. Semkiw, Walter, M.D. Historian Josephus www.Iisis.org
As accessed on November 19, 2017

7. Reincarnation, www.wikipedia.org
As accessed on November 19, 2017

10. Hubbard, Carol "Selections on Reincarnation History," www.reincarnationexperiment.org

As accessed on 3-5-2017

King, Martin Luther, "I've Been to the Mountain Top" as delivered on April 3, 1968, Mason Temple, Church of God in Christ Headquarters, Memphis, TN as accessed from www.Americanrhetoric.com/speeches/mlkivebeentoth emountaintop.htm on December 3, 2017

8. Connor, Miguel "Is Gnosticism a Reincarnation Religion," (Gospel of Phillip), September 29, 2016, the Gospel of Phillip as cited by Connor in Bringing Ancient Mysteries to a Modern Meaning www.thegodabovegod.com
As accessed on 3-20-2017

9. Connor, Miguel "Is Gnosticism a Reincarnation Religion," (Gospel of Thomas), September 29, 2016, the Gospel of Phillip as cited by Connor in Bringing Ancient Mysteries to a Modern Meaning www.thegodabovegod.com
As accessed on 3-20-2017

11. Semkiw, Walter, "Reincarnation and Past Lives," www.iisis.net
As accessed on 5-7-2017

12. Semkiw, Walter, "Dr. Ian Stevenson Past Life Stories with Physical Resemblance" www.iisis.net
As accessed on 5-7-2017

CPSIA information can be obtained
at www.ICGtesting.com
Printed in the USA
FSHW021034110320
68036FS